design bloggers
at home

design bloggers
at home

FRESH INTERIORS INSPIRATION FROM
LEADING ONLINE TREND-SETTERS

ELLIE TENNANT

photography by RACHEL WHITING

RYLAND PETERS & SMALL
LONDON • NEW YORK

DESIGNER Lucy Gowans and
Toni Kay

COMMISSIONING EDITOR
Stephanie Milner

LOCATION RESEARCH Jess Walton

PRODUCTION Meskerem Berhane

ART DIRECTOR Leslie Harrington

EDITORIAL DIRECTOR Julia Charles

STYLING Ellie Tennant

First published in 2014
by Ryland Peters & Small
20–21 Jockey's Fields,
London WC1R 4BW
and
519 Broadway, 5th Floor
New York, NY 10012
www.rylandpeters.com

10 9 8 7 6 5 4 3 2 1

ISBN 978-1-84975-507-8

Printed and bound in China

contents

introduction

Fuelled by Diet Coke and adrenalin, Rachel and I travelled the globe to make this book, visiting a gallimaufry of homes along the way. From a country ranch in rural California's Wild West to a smart seaside house in Sweden; from an ancient cottage in misty Cornwall, England, to an urban apartment in sunny San Francisco, USA – we covered many miles.

Despite the fact that we were taking trains, taxis and planes to reach each home – and having plenty of adventures along the way, from driving past Stonehenge in fog on midsummer solstice to flying low in a tiny propeller plane above bush fires in America – we were struck by how small the world of blogging really is. Online, there are no geographical barriers. No great distances. It's worth mentioning that all of the bloggers featured in this book were already friends with at least one of the others and it soon became clear that the world of interiors and design blogging is a close-knit, friendly community of passionate enthusiasts.

This was highlighted for us time and time again, not only by the connections and friendships that the bloggers we met had with one another, but by the kindness and generous hospitality that they showed to us as guests in their homes. From dashing around Target for a late-night, post-shoot shopping spree with Jonathan in California to enjoying Maria's freshly baked bread for lunch in Sacramento – the twelve bloggers in this book welcomed us into their homes and their lives; they gave us ice lollies when it was sweltering hot, they cooked us dinner, they gave us unexpected gifts, they drove us to and from airports and they were all, without exception, charming people to work and spend time with.

Dutch blogger Jane Schouten's love of the simple cross shape – a sign that conjures up First Aid to me, or, even worse, faint memories of dreaded maths lessons – keeps coming into my mind. It's an on-trend, ultra-cool design at the moment, of course reminiscent of vintage Swiss Army clobber and currently plastered across everything from contemporary monochrome blankets by Swedish textile artist Pia Wallén, to sculptural wall tiles by London ceramicist Lubna Chowdhary. But to Jane, it is a symbol of positivity – a plus.

Perhaps, then, it's appropriate that this simple but powerful shape features on the cushions in blogger Victoria Smith's San Francisco apartment, some 5,500 miles from Jane's house in the Netherlands. Maybe we can read it as a symbol of the nurturing, friendly, supportive global community of design bloggers. In these days of online fads, fashions and trends cross oceans and continents with ease. And so it seems, reassuringly, does friendship.

The bloggers in this book are among the cream of the crop, but there are many other brilliant blogs out there and a plethora of top bloggers with beautiful homes to explore. We simply couldn't fit them all in 160 pages. But online, there are no limitations, no boundaries. You don't need a passport, a visa or a plane ticket. Just sit back and log on – a whole world of inspiring interiors is awaiting your arrival.

pared back

style tip

Keep walls, cabinets, window dressings and appliances white to maximise the light in a kitchen – especially important during dark Swedish winters.

OPPOSITE The feeling of space and tranquillity in Niki's kitchen is enhanced by white-washed floorboards. 'We inherited high quality oak flooring and my husband wouldn't let me paint it,' she explains. 'I love black, white and wood together actually, so it all worked out well. Natural materials can really soften and warm up a monochrome scheme.'

LEFT A huge blackboard/chalkboard wall provides a gallery-like area where Niki displays her children's colourful artwork. 'They're only young once,' she says. 'I think it's sad when parents don't let their children self-express at home! It's also a handy place for me to stick shopping lists and write reminders.'

BELOW Niki is a talented artist and enjoys painting in her attic office, where she keeps her collection of paintbrushes in a vintage glass jar.

My Scandinavian Home

myscandinavianhome.blogspot.co.uk

The seaside home of English ex-pat Niki Brantmark is a light-filled family house that is both chic and practical. Spacious and sociable open-plan living areas have been cleverly zoned using lighting and furniture, and Niki is living proof that you can have a child-friendly home without sacrificing on style. Her look blends modern, Scandinavian design with a British, bohemian vibe. Antique, gold-gilded picture frames, reclaimed from an English art gallery, sit alongside monochrome, geometric accessories and arty screenprints by young, up-and-coming Danish, Dutch and Swedish designers. It's the perfect mix.

Niki's four-bedroom house was originally built in 2001 as a show home for the Bo01 housing exhibition, which focused on the regeneration of the docklands area of Malmö. 'The architects made this a lovely place to live,' she says. 'The roads are pedestrianized, so the children can play outside safely, there are communal gardens we share with neighbours and, wherever you are, you can hear running water, which gives the whole area a peaceful feel.'

ABOVE Pale pink sweet peas reflect Niki's 'girly' side. 'Swedish homes tend to be contemporary and masculine, but I sometimes dream of owning an old house full of romantic, vintage pieces,' she sighs.

LEFT Niki has transformed an upstairs bedroom into a 'TV snug'. The folk-style hemp cushions/pillows are by Finnish designer duo Saana Ja Olli. 'They take traditional designs and give them a modern twist,' Niki reveals.

It's idyllic, but when Niki, her Swedish husband, Per, and children, Olivia, Alice and Albin, first viewed the house five years ago, it wasn't exactly love at first sight. 'It had green ceilings and red skirting boards,' remembers Niki. 'It was horrific, actually. But the windows were massive and we loved the location, so we just went for it and painted all the walls and ceilings white as soon as we moved in.'

It might not sound like the most practical colour for family life, but Niki insists that white is surprisingly easy to live with. 'You can wash white walls with a damp sponge, so every now and again I get rid of all their [the children's] little fingerprints,' she laughs. 'Also, with white, you can easily touch-up areas or give walls another coat when you want a quick refresh. But I wouldn't have a white sofa, unless it had slipcovers. I draw the line at that.'

Apart from giving her home the airy, Scandinavian look she loves, the white walls also serve another important purpose. 'It gets really dark here during the

THIS PAGE 'I tend to blog all over the house, wherever I happen to be. Sometimes I blog in bed, or on the sofa downstairs,' says Niki. 'I use the desk upstairs to paint or work, because it's private and quiet.' Narrow ledges on the wall above provide the perfect place for Niki to display her favourite prints and photographs.

THIS PAGE The living area features vintage teak furniture, monochrome accessories and a hide rug. 'I love textures in a living room,' says Niki. 'I throw sheepskins over chairs, put rugs on the floor, scatter cushions/pillows and blankets everywhere; I hate that immaculate look — well, I don't hate it — I just can't do it!'

THIS PAGE Niki has nailed the art of display, arranging her treasures with skill and panache. 'My Single Diamond print is by up-and-coming graphic designer Katharina Berggreen,' reveals Niki, who is always on the look out for fresh art to add to her ever-growing collection. An industrial-style bare light bulb illuminates the display area, creating a focal point.

LEFT 'The hanging 1960s Bubble chair by Eero Aarnio used to be my little reading corner,' remembers Niki, 'but now the kids use it as a swing! We found it on the Swedish equivalent of eBay. When my husband went to pick it up, he phoned me to check that I really wanted it because it's such a statement piece.'

OPPOSITE, TOP LEFT Pretty clothes adorn the cupboard doors in the master bedroom. 'If you've got nice things, you shouldn't hide them away,' advises Niki. 'If I buy a cool pair of heels, I use them as styling props.'

OPPOSITE, BOTTOM LEFT Niki collects vintage glass perfume bottles. 'I like twinkly things,' she explains. She places them on the window sill so that they catch the light and bring some sparkle to the room.

OPPOSITE, FAR RIGHT The lofty master bedroom benefits from high ceilings, large windows and plenty of space. The bed is dressed simply but stylishly. 'I love linen sheets because they get softer the more you wash them,' says Niki. 'They improve with use and look good creased, which appeals to me.'

winter months when the sun barely rises and you never get a proper fix of sunlight. It's depressing,' explains Niki. 'That's why white walls and mirrors are so important here – to reflect as much light as possible.'

Unsurprisingly, good lighting is a priority and Niki has it down to a fine art. 'I've used lighting to divide our main living space into zones,' she says. 'The lights over the dining table are good task lights, I have an industrial-style bare bulb above a side table to illuminate it, practical

spotlights in the kitchen and reading lamps for a cosy glow in the living room.'

As long as you have clearly-defined areas, Niki believes that open-plan living makes family life fun and sociable. 'I can be cooking in the kitchen while one of the children is drawing at the table and another reading on the sofa – but we're all together and we can chat. It makes for a really warm family environment and works well when friends come over, too, as you're never hidden away in the

kitchen.' There is, however, one slight drawback: 'Per and I are both such messy cooks and we can't hide the chaos from our guests!'

By day, Niki works as Marketing Manager for an international communications company, but the blog she started to share her love of interior design is much more than just a hobby. 'I'm in a corporate world most of the time, so my blog provides escapism into a dream land full of things I'm passionate about,' she explains. 'In the evenings I'd much rather blog than watch TV and blogging has connected me to so many people around the world; it's really enriched my life.'

Blogging exposes Niki to images of inspiring houses every day. 'All the beautiful homes I see make me feel as though I constantly want to update our house,' she sighs. 'I feel under pressure when people come to visit now because they expect it to be really great – so that motivates me to tidy up!'

LEFT 'When we bought the bunk beds, there was a model with a slide in the shop, but we didn't go for that option, which was a bit unpopular with the kids,' recalls Niki. 'I love decorating their bedroom – I can introduce fun, colourful elements that I'd never have anywhere else in the house.'

OPPOSITE, TOP LEFT Cheery garlands made using fluorescent paper discs are strewn from shelves in the white-painted children's bedroom, bringing playful hits of bright colour to the space. Clutter is concealed inside neat stacks of pretty, patterned storage boxes.

OPPOSITE, TOP RIGHT Niki's stunning dandelion-style Maskros pendant light is from IKEA. 'I like to make changes all the time,' says Niki. 'I invest in a couple of expensive designer pieces, then pepper my home with more affordable bits that I can change on a regular basis.'

OPPOSITE, BOTTOM An eye-catching ornamental stag head gives the children's bedroom a fun feature. 'If I can look at a room and think it looks lovely, I'm instantly a bit happier,' says Niki.

Niki has perfected the art of achieving a clean, minimalist look while juggling family life. 'We've got good storage,' she confides. 'When you're a family as messy as we are, living in a country full of people as tidy as the Swedish are, it's essential. Everyone here has immaculate homes but you soon learn that they all have a secret drawer or cupboard where they hide their clutter.'

While her Swedish friends say they can sense Niki's 'Englishness' from her home, her English friends say her house looks Swedish. 'I think it's a mixture of the two cultures,' says Niki. 'A bit like me.'

OPPOSITE A glass-roofed, side-return extension floods Karine's airy family kitchen with light and creates space for a dining area. She displays her collection of elegant ceramics on an industrial shelving unit on castors. 'My home is constantly evolving, so I love portable pieces that I can easily move when I fancy,' says Karine.

RIGHT Dated, pine kitchen units have been updated and refreshed with a coat of blackboard/chalkboard paint, creating a striking, contemporary look. 'I want to replace the kitchen units eventually,' she explains, 'but in the meantime, this is a great temporary solution.'

BELOW Inspired by a London café, Karine's collection of antique silver cutlery/flatware is stored in vintage glass jars arranged in a group on the dining table.

Bodie and Fou

blog.bodieandfou.com

The London home of French boutique owner and blogger Karine Candice Köng is overflowing with creative styling ideas. By mixing old with new, she has retained the character of her charming, period townhouse, while creating a modern family home that's as effortlessly chic as it is warm and welcoming. Vintage treasures sit alongside sleek designer furniture, providing a canvas for Karine's ever-evolving, styled vignettes, while quirky finishing touches give every room her signature style.

Karine set up her online concept store, Bodie and Fou, with her sister Elodie in 2005 to bring their personal blend of French style to a worldwide audience. The shop is named after the sisters' nicknames for each other – Elodie is 'Bodie' and Karine is 'Fou.'

Good design runs in her blood. She grew up in a creative environment with a father who loved DIY and a mother who spent her weekends sewing. They took her to flea markets and her lifelong love affair with interiors began at an early age.

style tip

Maximise space and light
in a room by painting all
the walls white and laying pale
stone floor tiles throughout
for an airy feel

THIS PAGE Karine's eye for detail and her talent for the art of display are evident in her living room, where a monochrome theme dominates. The marble mantelpiece provides a platform for Karine to arrange her *objets trouvés*, while a wall inside one alcove is plastered with black and white art prints and family photos, all fixed to the wall with Japanese Washi masking tape.

DO what
you think
is RiGHT

'I love to constantly refresh my home,
so I always keep a roll of black masking
tape to hand and make mini mood
boards on the walls.'

THIS IS TAPE!

536

LEFT 'When we were house-hunting, within two minutes of walking in through the front door, I knew this was the house for us,' reveals Karine. 'The hallway floor tiles were already here, but they're perfect for me because they're black and white.' Karine has concealed the radiator inside a chic cover, that also provides a useful ledge.

Karine's blog – or 'Le Blog' as she affectionately calls it – started life a year later, as a channel to promote the sisters' shop. But it soon became a virtual scrapbook in which to share her inspirations, her passion for fashion and her interior design ideas. It is now considered a 'little black book of interiors' by the likes of *Vogue* magazine, features everything from motivational and poetic quotations to stunning photographs of her home, and has become a one-stop-shop for design enthusiasts.

'My blog very quickly became about much more than just my business,' muses Karine. 'It's almost like a diary to me and very personal. It's a way for me to share my passion for interior decoration online with other enthusiasts, but it's also an important creative virtual space, where I can explore ideas and designs.'

Karine feels that writing a blog has broadened her horizons. 'I used to read a lot of same-y French interiors magazines, but now I read titles such as *VT Wonen* from Holland and *Inside Out* from Australia – I'm exposed to a much wider range of styles and trends.'

When Karine first viewed the four-bedroom, Victorian home she shares with her husband, Steve, and daughter, Mila, she immediately sensed it was 'the one'. 'It was the sense of space that first attracted me to this house,' she says.

ABOVE Karine has painted her daughter's wardrobe/closet doors in a classic, pale grey colour, but has added a slick of fuchsia pink paint to the door edges for an unexpected detail.

LEFT Her daughter Mila's bedroom was the first room that Karine decorated when the family moved in. 'It's still my favourite room,' she says. 'I would never decorate in a girly, pink colour – I much prefer grey. When we moved in, the walls were yellow, the shelves were pale green and the floorboards were dark brown, so I've freshened it up with white floorboards and a smart dark grey wall. I love painting. There is instant gratification when you do it.'

'We were just about to give up on house hunting. We'd seen so many and none of them were quite right. This one was the last we saw and it was perfect – just a ten-minute cycle from Notting Hill and in a leafy, village-like area of the city.'

Karine has decorated the house throughout with white, but warm natural materials such as leather, marble and wood prevent the rooms from feeling stark or cold. 'I love

mixing different textures together and incorporating organic materials that have integrity,' explains Karine. 'I always find beauty in natural objects. For example, I pick up bits of wood at the beach and bring them home to display them. I like shells, too. My look is pared back and edited, so each object I own has a story behind it.'

Her rooms are effortlessly chic – a beguiling cocktail of vintage treasures, contemporary, designer buys and

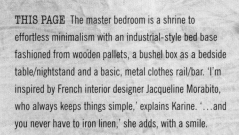

THIS PAGE The master bedroom is a shrine to effortless minimalism with an industrial-style bed base fashioned from wooden pallets, a bushel box as a bedside table/nightstand and a basic, metal clothes rail/bar. 'I'm inspired by French interior designer Jacqueline Morabito, who always keeps things simple,' explains Karine. '…and you never have to iron linen,' she adds, with a smile.

THIS PAGE Karine has used simple strips of black Japanese Washi masking tape on the hall walls to frame a chic display of vintage finds and graphic, monochrome art prints. Her French market basket is always close to hand.

OPPOSITE, TOP Delicate rosaries hang from the corner of an antique mirror in Karine's bedroom. 'I've always liked crosses,' she explains. 'My husband gave me a beautiful rosary from New Zealand once, made from volcanic stone.'

OPPOSITE, BOTTOM LEFT Many of the accessories and art prints in Karine's home are stocked in her online shop. 'I bring things home to photograph them for our catalogue and fall in love with them,' she laughs.

OPPOSITE, BOTTOM RIGHT Even Karine's lighting is pared-back and timelessly stylish; a sculptural, contemporary 'Cluster' light by British ceramicist Kathleen Hills hangs in Karine's bedroom and looks particularly beautiful against the white-painted walls and ornate plaster cornicing on the ceiling.

carefully-chosen, high street finds. 'I love IKEA,' she admits, 'but I'm selective. It's like fashion; if you mix expensive designer pieces with high street bargains, it works.'

Karine's inspiring less-is-more approach extends to every area of her home. 'You just don't need much stuff,' she insists. 'In your kitchen, if you have a simple, rustic wooden table, a little jug and a small bunch of flowers, that's it. You're sorted.'

Despite her penchant for monochrome interiors, Karine isn't afraid to throw splashes of colour into the mix here and there. Her linen bed sheets are a bright turquoise blue. 'I've always wanted to create a home that has a laid-back, holiday-like feel,' explains Karine. 'Turquoise reminds me of the sky and sea, while natural linen conjures up memories of summer days at the beach. It gives the room a really relaxed feel.'

Karine loves:

• **Instagram**, instagram.com. It's visual, which suits me.
• **Garance Doré**, garancedore.fr. I prefer reading fashion blogs.

SHOPS:

• **Chez Les Voisins,** chezlesvoisins.fr.
• **Les Petits Bohemes,** lespetitsbohemes.bigcartel.com.
• **L'Atelier du Petit Parc,** atelierdupetitparc.fr.

Top blogging tips:

• Relax and just be yourself. That's when you really tap into your own creativity and do your best work – when you just do your own thing, rather than trying to emulate a blog that you like. I did my blog originally because it's good for the business, but I've always written from the heart.

• Keep things real and personal. As well as sharing photos of my home and my design finds, I post about simplifying my home life, my yoga challenges, my family and health. The personal posts are always the most popular.

• Keep at it – you'll get there. It can take a while to find your voice, but don't give up.

OPPOSITE Desiree has painted a dramatic black feature wall in her kitchen. 'It's only paint,' she shrugs. 'People get so nervous about painting walls in dark, theatrical colours, but I say: just do it. If you don't like it, you can always just paint over it. Paint is only temporary, so have some fun with it.'

RIGHT Rustic concrete bowls and sleek black ceramics are stacked around Desiree's tidy kitchen. 'I love it in here,' she says. 'I tend to blog at the kitchen table these days more than at my desk.'

Vosges Paris

vosgesparis.blogspot.co.uk

The Amsterdam apartment of stylish blogger Desiree Groenendal is a peaceful oasis, tucked away from the hustle and bustle of city life. With clean, white walls, exposed, concrete panels and generous proportions, her ground floor flat feels more like an airy loft, thanks to some savvy decorating decisions. Hers is an impressively disciplined existence; the colours black and white are strictly adhered to throughout, resulting in a dramatic interior that's filled with photogenic arrangements at every turn. It's perfection, but her clever use of textures, combined with her kind heart, makes this elegant home feel friendly. Whether she's busy arranging (or rearranging) artistic clusters of photographs, prints and inspirational quotations on her gallery-style walls, or making a designer-style hanging clothes rail/bar for her minimalist bedroom, social worker Desiree's stunning home is much more than just a place to live; it's a labour of love.

It was 23 years ago that Desiree bought her new-build apartment in the former docklands of east Amsterdam. It's an area rich in history and character, where ships laden with cocoa and tea used to deliver their goods to warehouses in the nearby harbour. 'There's water all around,' says Desiree. 'That's partly why I like it here. It feels tranquil.'

Her building is a modern, concrete block – anonymous and unremarkable from the outside, perhaps, but the perfect blank canvas inside for her to transform. 'Rather unromantically, it was built on the site of a former slaughter house, so they used to kill cows here,' reveals Desiree. 'Luckily, my flat is on the ground floor where the staff canteen used to be!'

THIS PAGE At the centre of Desiree's immaculate monochrome kitchen is a framed quotation. 'It's my mantra: Get the best out of life – do things you like and make the most of every day,' she says, smiling.

THIS IS YOUR **LIFE.**
DO WHAT YOU LOVE,
AND DO IT OFTEN.
IF YOU DON'T LIKE SOMETHING, CHANGE IT.
IF YOU DON'T LIKE YOUR JOB, QUIT.
IF YOU DON'T HAVE ENOUGH TIME, STOP WATCHING TV.
IF YOU ARE LOOKING FOR THE LOVE OF YOUR LIFE, STOP;
THEY WILL BE WAITING FOR YOU WHEN YOU
START DOING THINGS YOU LOVE.
STOP OVER ANALYZING, ALL EMOTIONS ARE BEAUTIFUL.
LIFE IS SIMPLE. WHEN YOU EAT, APPRECIATE
EVERY LAST BITE.
OPEN YOUR MIND, ARMS, AND HEART TO NEW THINGS
AND PEOPLE, WE ARE UNITED IN OUR DIFFERENCES.
ASK THE NEXT PERSON YOU SEE WHAT THEIR PASSION IS,
AND SHARE YOUR INSPIRING DREAM WITH THEM.
TRAVEL OFTEN; GETTING LOST WILL
HELP YOU FIND YOURSELF.
SOME OPPORTUNITIES ONLY COME ONCE, SEIZE THEM.
LIFE IS ABOUT THE PEOPLE YOU MEET, AND
THE THINGS YOU CREATE WITH THEM
SO GO OUT AND START CREATING.
LIFE IS LIVE YOUR DREAM,
SHORT. AND WEAR
YOUR PASSION.

"Style is
a way to
say who you
are without
having to
speak."

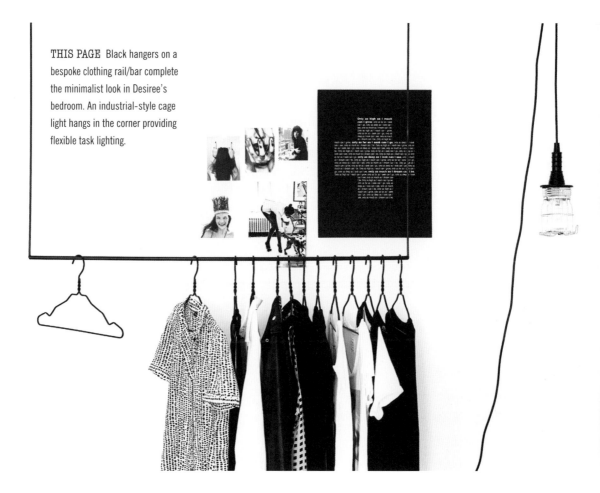

THIS PAGE Black hangers on a bespoke clothing rail/bar complete the minimalist look in Desiree's bedroom. An industrial-style cage light hangs in the corner providing flexible task lighting.

OPPOSITE, TOP LEFT Desiree's extensive collection of plain, white tableware is displayed inside her black-painted, 'up-cycled' armoire.

OPPOSITE, TOP RIGHT In the office, a desk has been made from a reclaimed beer festival table, painted white. 'It's been outside for years, so it has a beautiful patina,' says Desiree.

OPPOSITE, BOTTOM RIGHT Regimented grids of Polaroid snaps create intriguing, artistic vignettes on Desiree's crisp, white walls.

OPPOSITE, BOTTOM LEFT Framed motivational quotations provide constant inspiration around Desiree's beautiful home.

When her children moved out, she decided to make some changes. 'I knocked down walls and removed door frames to open the space up and make it feel much larger,' she explains. These simple structural alterations gave Desiree a completely new home. 'The flat suddenly felt contemporary and Scandinavian – light and airy. My neighbours were shocked when they first saw it.'

All the walls were covered with wallpaper when she moved in. 'One day, I peeled off a little corner and found this amazing concrete underneath,' says Desiree, gleefully. 'I loved the texture so much that I exposed sections all around the flat for an industrial, edgy look.' Next, she painted all the walls white and used masking tape to frame her raw concrete feature panels with smart borders.

The resulting squares provide the perfect rough, textured backdrop for her pop-up moodboards, which come and go throughout the year, changing the look of her apartment whenever she fancies. 'I use Japanese Washi tape and bull dog clips for temporary displays and my choices are often seasonal,' says

Desiree. 'If it's summer, I'll include photos of people on beaches or in the sunshine – images that capture the mood of the moment.'

In the kitchen, a grid of nine black and white Polaroid snaps provides a striking feature on an otherwise plain wall, while in the living room, wooden-framed art canvases are used as pin boards for Desiree's latest tear-sheet collections. 'My home is like a playground, where I constantly explore and try out new things,' she explains. Even the darkest corner of the hallway has been turned into a visual triumph, with a stunning neon light above rows of inspiring photographs.

'I don't know whether my home influences my blog, or my blog influences my home,' says Desiree, thoughtfully. 'I see so many inspiring interiors online that I'm always changing my house as a result, but I don't do things at home just so that I can blog about it. It's an organic process but I'm probably a bit more organised about my home

ABOVE Desiree's simple living room is further evidence of her impressive restraint, with just a few, cherished pieces of furniture and selected accessories. 'I love my grey floors,' she says. 'White floors can be a bit harsh – but grey gives a softer look and links the contrasting black and white elements in my home together.'

RIGHT Desiree loves her Japanese Washi tape designed by Paola Navone. 'If I like a photo, I just grab some tape and stick it straight on the wall,' she says. 'I don't use many frames.' She uses a retro handheld Dymo labelling machine to label her office supplies and filing systems with black and white adhesive stickers.

OPPOSITE, TOP LEFT Like the other 'Pared Back' bloggers in this book, Desiree favours pure linen bed linen. 'It oozes nonchalance,' she says. 'It's low maintenance, casual and informal – what's not to love?' The vintage school lockers were a gift from a friend, customized with fabric organisers so they're practical for clothes storage.

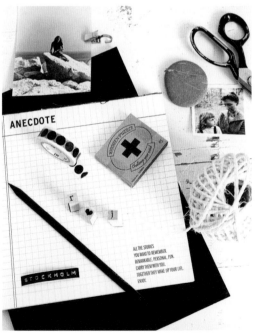

ABOVE In her bedroom, an Eiffel Tower ornament and a monochrome French road sign are clues to Desiree's passion for all things Parisian. 'My favourite shop is Merci in Paris,' she says, dreamily.

projects, because I want to document them, than I would be if I didn't blog.'

'Blogging is an important part of my life now,' says Desiree. 'It's like brushing my teeth before I leave the house – a part of my daily routine.' Although she is always thinking about her blog, it never becomes a chore. 'It's always at the back of my mind,' she says. 'I'm always mulling over my last post or planning the next, but I never feel pressurised into blogging. I love it.'

Desiree started blogging back in 2008, after months of making plans. 'I couldn't come up with a good name, so I just used my Gmail username: Vosges Paris,' she reveals. It's a fitting title for her blog though, as she is

a self-confessed Francophile who loves Parisian style and enjoys mixing French greys with Scandinavian whites to create her own look.

Although her home looks polished and expensive, Desiree is a thrifty up-cycler who knows how to get a designer look without spending too much. Having admired a sleek hanging clothes rail/bar in Paris, she headed home and immediately mocked one up in her bedroom using masking tape to find the perfect dimensions and position, then took her measurements to a local blacksmith and asked him to make it for her. 'I painted it black and that was that,' she says with a smile. 'It's my most precious possession but didn't cost much at all.'

On the chalkboard armoire: *When you eat appreciate life every last bit... open your mind, arms and heart to things and people, we are united... differences. Ask the next person what your inspiration is and share your inspiration with them. Travel often; getting lost helps you find yourself. Some things will only come once, seize... is all about the people you meet and the things you create with them. Get out and start creating... live your dream and live your passion*

VOSGESPARIS.COM

LEFT An armoire painted in blackboard/chalkboard paint is an example of Desiree's creativity and DIY expertise. Lovingly reclaimed and revived, it now provides a useful surface to write reminders or inspirational phrases on. It's a hit with her readers. 'The most popular posts on my blog are always the ones when people see a little slice of my life,' she says.

OPPOSITE, TOP LEFT By cleverly removing doors and door frames throughout her apartment, Desiree has created the illusion of a loft-style and warehouse-esque space with high ceilings and plenty of natural daylight. It's clean, contemporary and spacious.

OPPOSITE, TOP RIGHT Plain art canvases are propped against the living room walls, providing a display area for Desiree's pop-up moodboards and favourite photos. 'I want to change something in the living room, but I don't know what yet!' she laughs.

OPPOSITE, BOTTOM The tiles on Desiree's kitchen trolley are from *VT Wonen* magazine. 'They're perfect for my home, so I collected lots. I just love graphic circles.'

Another example of her ingenuity is the chic, black armoire in her dining area. 'It was 50 cents,' chuckles Desiree. 'I bought it from my children's school years ago and it was originally dark blue. It took me three weeks to clean it.' Years later, when she tired of it, she thought about throwing it away, but instead, sanded it down and coated it with blackboard/ chalkboard paint. 'I fell in love with it all over again,' she recalls. 'Now I have so much fun writing on it with chalk and it makes my collection of white tableware look really stunning.'

ART CANVASES.

Desiree loves:

• **Feedly**, feedly.com. I use this online news reader tool to organize my favourite blogs.

SHOPS:

• **La Maison d'Anna G**, lamaisondannag.com.

• **Merci**, merci-merci.com.

• **VT Wonen Shop**, vtwonenshop.nl.

Top blogging tips:

• Blogging is a journey. Once you start, you will gradually find your own way.

• Be yourself. Just write naturally and don't try to emulate others who you admire. Don't try to be someone you're not. Try to be original.

rustic

CORNISH
FAIRINGS
SPICED BISCUIT

NET WT 11 1/2 oz 326g
A Cornish Speciality

HOVIS

OPPOSITE Rebecca uses charcoal grey linen (bought by the metre/yard) as a tablecloth and displays storage jars and simple pottery on her enormous Welsh dresser, which she bought on eBay and painted coral pink. Above the antique table hangs a contemporary, industrial-style pendant light. 'I'm always trying to strike a balance between modern and rustic,' explains Rebecca.

LEFT A terracotta jug/pitcher filled with fresh garden flowers sits beside a sea urchin on the kitchen window sill. 'I'm drawn to natural forms,' says Rebecca. 'I collected this sea urchin at the beach and I like the idea of nature tables. My daughter, Wren, keeps bringing feathers home.'

BELOW Thick, oak worksurfaces, vintage, wooden storage crates, chunky chopping boards and platter-like, hand-turned acacia plates give Rebecca's kitchen a reassuringly warm, artisanal look.

Futurustic

futurusticblog.com

By combining craft makes with vintage finds and modern buys, blogger Rebecca Proctor has managed to fuse all the strands of her various passions together to make her Cornish coastal cottage a contemporary family home. Her blog, Futurustic, marries her love of cutting-edge design with her penchant for a more traditional, rustic approach to home-making. Few could blend such opposing looks so seamlessly, but the hours of hard graft that Rebecca and her partner, Andrew, have put into perfecting their country home prove that, with a thrifty approach, some DIY skills and a lot of imagination, you can achieve anything.

When design writer Rebecca and her partner, illustrator Andrew, left London five years ago to move to the Cornish coast, they were looking for a project. The house they fell for was just ten minutes away from the beach and enjoyed a secluded position overlooking picturesque farmland.

'It was originally two separate cottages, dating from around 1780,' explains Rebecca. 'When we moved in, it was still divided into lots of little rooms and felt dark and cramped, so the first thing we did was knock down lots of walls to open the space up and flood the house with light.'

style tip

Hang a metal pendant
on an adjustable long length
of cable, so you can easily
lower the light for a cosy glow
when dining.

'I love winter here. We snuggle up, play board games and drink hot chocolate beside the stove.'

LEFT The living room walls are clad in floor-to-ceiling, tongue-and-groove wood panelling, painted in a soft, putty grey shade for a country, coastal look. 'I like muted colours,' says Rebecca. 'We painted everything white first, but we soon realised that it looked dirty really quickly, so we re-painted everything using a much greyer palette.'

OPPOSITE By papering a wall with pages cut from vintage *Boys' Own* annuals, Rebecca has brought character and interest to the cottage's small landing space. A retro wicker chair provides a comfy place to read while the fun penguin pattern on the cushion/pillow is echoed in the homemade hanging paper bird mobile above.

Precious original features such as flagstone flooring, exposed brickwork and inglenook fireplaces have all been retained, but modern additions such as Danish Morsø wood-burning stoves and a new kitchen have been tastefully incorporated to update the home for 21st-century living.

After city life, the refreshingly wild and untamed Cornish landscape appealed to the couple. 'Life feels very free and easy here. We're surrounded by nature and it's a great place to bring up children.' But despite the many advantages of living in a rural, remote area, Rebecca admits she can sometimes feel a little isolated. 'One of the upsides of blogging it that it's made me feel much more connected to the rest of the country and the whole world. I'm part of an online design community, which keeps me in the loop, despite my location.'

Rebecca started blogging four years ago with a private blog that nobody knew about. 'I didn't really take to it and I didn't really know why I was doing it,' she confides. When her daughter, Wren, was born, she started blogging in earnest and launched Futurustic. 'I realised that I was practically blogging anyway on my own computer, but nobody was seeing it. I had loads of folders on my desktop which were all potential blog posts, so it just made sense for me to share it all online.'

Having worked as a trend forecaster and authored books about sustainable living, Rebecca found her blog gave her a virtual space in which to explore her creativity, while she and Andrew put the rest of their energies into doing up their home.

'Luckily, Andrew is a talented carpenter,' says Rebecca, with a smile. Evidence of his endeavours is all around the house, from carefully-crafted wooden shutters at the windows to elegant photo frames made from driftwood picked up on the local beach. The finish is as good as any professional could ever hope to achieve.

Meanwhile, Rebecca put her own decorating talents to good use; 'I used the pages from a vintage *Boys' Own* annual to wallpaper the landing wall, sewed bunting for

LEFT Rebecca is an expert at mixing the old with the new; on the sofa, homemade cushion/pillow covers crafted from a vintage, Welsh woollen blanket sit next to modern, monochrome, geometric mud cloth designs. Skilful Andrew made the rustic, wooden coffee table and the colourful antique rug is a family hand-me-down that blends into the room beautifully.

OPPOSITE, TOP LEFT A painted peg rail provides useful storage space in the compact children's bedroom. Rebecca uses the shelf above to display pretty, vintage children's books picked up at car boot sales.

OPPOSITE, TOP RIGHT AND BOTTOM LEFT Rebecca decorated the bedroom walls with a patterned roller. 'It's a really easy alternative to wallpaper and only took a couple of hours,' she reveals.

OPPOSITE, BOTTOM RIGHT When she was choosing pages from old books for her landing wall, Rebecca carefully selected those with the most interesting illustrations and stories. Tradtional Bakelite light switches give a pleasingly vintage look.

LEFT A vintage French classroom poster depicting *plantes sans fleurs* hangs above the bed in the master bedroom and a potted plant on the bedside table/nightstand subtly echoes the illustrations. The simple bedlinen is from Toast, a British brand that captures Rebecca's favourite blend of country and modern.

OPPOSITE, BOTTOM LEFT Colourful lengths of bunting made from fabric remnants are draped around the children's bedroom walls. The bird quilt was sewn by Rebecca and Andrew fitted narrow ledges to the walls to prop the kids' favourite books on. Sash windows and wooden shutters give each room a timeless, country feel.

OPPOSITE, BOTTOM RIGHT Rebecca made the illustrative shower curtain in the bathroom herself and painted the cast iron, rolltop tub with claw feet in Pigeon Grey, by Farrow & Ball. 'Andrew made the wooden bathtub rack from driftwood he collected on the beach,' says Rebecca. 'It's just weathered scrap timber, but great for making things, and free.'

OPPOSITE, TOP Some of her neighbours in the village sell fresh flowers grown in their gardens, so Rebecca enjoys beautiful blooms around the house all year round.

the children's bedroom using old silk scraps and updated a second-hand Welsh dresser in the kitchen with a coat of coral paint,' she says. 'I'm a great believer in recycling and we prefer to make things for our home than buy them wherever possible. It's cheaper and more fun.'

As well as being talented creatives, Rebecca and Andrew are keen vintage hunters, always keeping their eyes open for quirky treasures. Sometimes, being observant pays off; 'a while ago, a man in the village was preparing for a bonfire and had a huge stack of scrap wood in his garden,' recalls Rebecca. 'We spotted some

beautiful vintage crates on top of the heap, so did a swap with him and exchanged a bag of logs for them. The amazing Norwegian Skippers box in our kitchen was one of those we rescued. He must have thought we were mad!'

Their electrician certainly did. 'When we moved in, there were beautiful Bakelite light switches in every room,' says Rebecca, with a smile. 'Our electrician sadly had to remove them because they didn't meet safety regulations, but I loved them so much that I spent a small fortune on replica ones. He thought it was completely bonkers, but sometimes, it's the details that matter.'

Rebecca loves:

- **Ledansla**, ledansla.blogspot.co.uk.
- **Tomboy Style**, tomboystyle.blogspot.co.uk.
- **101 Cookbooks**, 101cookbooks.com.
- **Instagram**, instagram.com.
- **Bloglovin**, bloglovin.com.

SHOPS:

- **The New Craftsmen,** thenewcraftsmen.myshopify.com.
- **Fine Little Day,** shop.finelittleday.com.
- **Herriott Grace,** shop.herriottgrace.com.
- **Couverture & The Garbstore,** couvertureandthegarbstore.com.

Top blogging tips:

- Tell people about your blog and promote it. With the pressure of an audience, you will feel motivated to produce regular content.
- I follow lots of blogs using the Bloglovin tool. It sends you an email every day with all the new posts from your favourite blogs. You can add a button to your browser bar and it shows you how many new posts there are to read every day. It's addictive!
- Instagram is great used in moderation. Some bloggers put about 20 pictures up on it every day. Personally, I like to see more blog content, but it's whatever works for you.

Dreamy Whites

dreamywhites.blogspot.co.uk

Self-confessed antiques addict Maria Carr blogs about recreating French farmhouse style on a ranch in northern California. Surrounded by fruit trees and rolling fields, her airy home is a new-build, but feels much older thanks to vintage furniture and antique architectural elements – the perfect backdrop for Maria's ever-expanding array of French finds. On her blog, beautiful photography not only captures her elegant interior style, it also conveys a real sense of her simple life on the ranch, which she shares with her five children and her 'handsome cowboy' husband, not to mention a plethora of pets. One minute she's baking a blueberry pie, the next she's home-schooling her kids, blogging about paint colours, packing up products or driving to a flea market to hunt for more vintage loveliness.

It's hard to believe that Maria's home arrived on a lorry in three parts just seven years ago. 'It's a kit,' she explains. 'It's a single storey design – we joined three kits together so we could have plenty of space.' To give the building some character, her husband fitted a wood-burning stove, added ornate moulded trims to the windows and fixed reclaimed

OPPOSITE Maria's painted French armoire is filled with vintage jars, cake stands, jugs/pitchers and bowls. 'It was originally a built-in cupboard,' she explains. 'Consequently, it had one side missing, so I had to fix it and paint the new side blue to match.'

LEFT Suspended on ropes above the kitchen table, a quirky chandelier made from reclaimed wooden planks and vintage glass preserving jars provides a striking focal point. Folding bistro chairs in cheery colours give Maria's dining area an eclectic, relaxed feel.

ABOVE LEFT Vintage French Moutarde de Maille mustard pots, picked up at flea markets, sit alongside contemporary numbered spice jars in Maria's heavenly wire-fronted armoire.

ABOVE Neat rows of leather boots line the family's ranch hallway. 'My kids are farm kids,' says Maria, 'so, we have lots of boots for riding, working and walking.'

LEFT Maria loves vintage pieces of furniture that have interesting stories to tell – especially this little table, which has peeling layers of faded old newspaper stories literally stuck to its surface.

tin tiles to the walls and ceiling of the living room. 'I love our home, but I've always dreamed of living in an older house,' says Maria, with a smile. 'It's brand new, but I've tried to give it personality.'

She's succeeded, by filling the house with her château-chic treasures; enamel jugs are artfully-arranged inside distressed wooden cupboards, white sofas with slipcovers are piled with plump cushions/pillows made from vintage ticking linens, while raw wooden doors and shutters are propped up against pale, French-grey walls.

It has all the grandeur and elegance of a Provence farmhouse – but with the generous proportions and modern conveniences of a Californian ranch home.

French-inspired interiors can sometimes feel saccharine, but, by adding recycled and industrial pieces such as metal bistro chairs and rustic bushel boxes and avoiding flouncy 'frou frou' florals, Maria has ensured her home is far from twee. Instead, it's a flawless combination of the utilitarian and the romantic – a working family home, with a lovely but laid-back vibe.

THIS PAGE An enormous dresser in the living room houses Maria's extensive collections of cookery books and tableware. A glittering antique chandelier brings a touch of French glamour to the space, while dainty antique armchairs with soft, linen covers give the room a romantic, shabby-chic ambience.

THIS PAGE By fitting reclaimed tin tiles to the walls, Maria has given her new-build home character and warmth. 'They needed painting but I loved the pattern,' says Maria. 'In the winter, we huddle in this corner because it's so cosy. We had this stove in our last home and brought it with us when we moved here.'

'I love raw, faded wood and interesting textures with history,' Maria says. 'I found a little table once with old newspaper stuck to the top of it. The news print had become part of the surface of the tabletop and it had a fabulous patina. I like to imagine who owned an item before me – what they did, where they lived.'

This fascination with yesteryear started when Maria was just a teenager, growing up on a remote prairie dairy farm in rural Montana. 'I had a job renovating old furniture for a local shop,' she explains. 'I've been passionate about antiques ever since.'

THIS PAGE Maria's home is a hub of creative activity where nothing is wasted. Big baskets filled with linen remnants are evidence of Maria's thrifty approach to craft; 'when we make bags or cushion/pillow covers, we sew little lavender bags from the leftover fabric scraps and include them in packages we send out to customers,' she says.

LEFT 'I have an obsession with doors,' confesses Maria. 'I like faded, aged wood that's lost its paint and has a natural grain.' Two old doors propped casually against the bedroom wall create an elegant headboard and lend an air of history to the new building. Soft, white, linen bedlinen, an antique chest and a stunning chandelier complete the look.

OPPOSITE By leaning old wooden shutters against the wall, stylish Maria successfully manages to give her American home an authentic French flavour. Vintage blue, white and red linens are hung in an open-fronted cupboard that's part storage, part display. Instead of hanging art on the walls, Maria prefers to temporarily fix her favourite prints to shutters and doors with rustic pegs and simply swaps them around when she wants to refresh her look.

When a total stranger casually suggested to Maria that she could start a blog, she had 'no expectations'. In fact, she didn't know much about blogging at all, or imagine it could lead to a new enterprise for her. 'I started it on a whim and had no idea that there was a whole network of bloggers out there,' she recalls. 'I just began to document my ideas online and share my love of antiques with others. When people started to ask me where I bought the things in my home, I thought I might as well start selling them, so my blog inspired my online shop.'

Maria, a shy, sweet woman, is still surprised by her own success. 'Blogging has had such a positive impact on my life, I feel truly blessed,' she says, with emotion. 'I've met some incredible people online and the opportunities I've been given because of the blog are amazing. I never expected any of it.'

Her home is constantly evolving as her tastes change, and it is only fairly recently that Maria started to introduce subtle coloured elements to her home, preferring before to keep her scheme all white. 'I was a bit afraid of adding

colour,' she admits. 'When we moved in, I painted all the walls pure, brilliant white, but, because we have huge windows, it was harsh and a bit cold. It felt as though something was missing.'

Now, the walls are a putty grey shade. 'It feels so much warmer,' says Maria, happily. 'I bought a pale blue armoire for our dining area and it looked so lovely that I soon got over my phobia of colour.'

Fresh flowers also introduce cheery hues to Maria's rooms. 'I planted lots of wild roses and hydrangeas outside the back door when we moved here, so I could pick them for the house without feeling guilty. I hate picking flowers that are blooming when there are only a few there,' she explains. 'But the plants grew way bigger than I ever expected them to and now we always have some indoors.'

OPPOSITE, TOP LEFT 'I have a real thing for old chopping boards at the moment,' says Maria. 'They're so rustic and they improve with age the more you use them.' Thanks to the mild Californian climate, fresh figs are always readily available locally.

OPPOSITE, TOP RIGHT Even though she lives in a single-storey home, Maria has a large section of reclaimed staircase in the corner of her hallway. 'It's just a prop for displaying shop products on but I've always wanted a second floor!' laughs Maria.

OPPOSITE, BOTTOM LEFT Small ceramic bottles fill a painted bedroom cabinet. Despite her huge collection of vintage finds, Maria's home does not feel cluttered, thanks to careful editing and restrained displays; she knows that less is often more.

THIS PAGE 'I'm always drawn to blue glass – it's an ongoing collection,' admits Maria, who owns an impressive array of turquoise glass containers, from French La Lorraine bottles to American Blue Ball Mason jars. She displays them on a marble-topped folding table and lines them up next to windows.

Maria loves:

- **Miss Mustard Seed**, missmustardseed.com. Miss Mustard Seed was one of the first people to ask me to guest post for her. She is driven and inspires me to keep going.
- **Blogger**, blogger.com.

SHOPS:

- **Maison Rêve,** maisonreve.com.
- **Sadie Olive,** sadieolive.com. The owner, Sara Duckett, takes gorgeous photographs.
- **Anthropologie,** anthropologie.com. I love the handmade homewares at this shop.

Top blogging tips:

- Stay true to who you are; just do your own thing. It can be a bit overwhelming at first — you're suddenly connected to so many people. Don't have any expectations — start without an agenda.
- Love what you post about.

retro chic

OPPOSITE Victoria's dining room is an eclectic mix of vintage pieces and cutting-edge designs. 'I considered painting the table white once but I'm so glad I didn't,' she says. Victoria's an expert at mixing different wood finishes together – rich, honey-coloured floorboards, a dark, stained table and a pale, stripped-back sideboard all sit together harmoniously.

LEFT The sociable open-plan kitchen is home to Victoria's enviable collection of kitchenalia – a gallimaufry of simply chic ceramic, wood and glass pieces, which look beautiful against the warm wooden kitchen units and sleek black worksurfaces. The designer chair echoes these materials, linking the living room and the kitchen together visually.

BELOW LEFT A group of mid-century modern, Danish teak candlesticks makes an attractive display on the dining room sideboard.

SF Girl by Bay

sfgirlbybay.com

Set back from the road, tucked away in a verdant courtyard in San Francisco's famously sunny Noe Valley quarter, is Victoria Smith's stylish and homely apartment where she lives with her dog, Lucy. It's in a smart, early 1900s building, covered with purple blooms, which dangle and dance in front of the windows. Inside, flea market finds blend with cutting-edge contemporary designs to create a look that's fresh but also friendly. Her one-bedroom rental is not a big space, but Victoria is a talented curator, editing her possessions with care and arranging them with such affection that the flat feels not only spacious, but welcoming too.

Before Victoria moved in, she asked her landlord to make some changes. 'The walls were beige and the rooms were carpeted,' she remembers, 'so I had all the walls painted white and got the carpets ripped up to reveal the wooden flooring underneath. I removed the concertina door that separated the living room from the dining room too, which made the space open-plan and much more sociable. I wanted to get rid of the pillar as well, but it was holding the ceiling up so had to stay! Now, it's a great place to entertain friends and I'm very happy here.'

ABOVE Victoria loves pink Dahlias – the official flower of San Francisco – arranged in a shallow, teak bowl. 'I go to the market on Friday so I have fresh flowers for the weekend. It's always inspiring to wander through the stalls,' she says.

LEFT A vintage-style Crosley record player brings a retro flavour to Victoria's airy dining room. Her vinyl collection is kept conveniently close-by for old-fashioned background music when she has friends over for dinner.

Before she became a full-time blogger, Victoria worked as an art buyer and print producer at an advertising agency, where she learnt creative skills that often come in handy in her new career. 'My background helps me so much, because I have a critical eye and I know what makes a good picture,' she explains.

In 2006, Victoria 'didn't know what a blog was', but a friend encouraged her to start her own. She used her email username – SFGirlbybay – and things soon started to snowball. Today, she has over 25,000 readers a day and blogging has completely transformed her life. 'I don't

have to get up at the crack of dawn and do a nine-to-five office job anymore,' she says, with a smile. 'Although my job is still stressful, it's all on my own terms. I create my own deadlines which gives me the freedom to spend more time doing the things I love.'

Her life and her blog now intersect. 'If I go to a gallery or out shopping with a friend, I'm always thinking: this could be a good blog post!' she chuckles. She's constantly scouring websites for new ideas. 'My look changes all the time. Right now I'm into white and wood,' she says. 'I like shapes and textures much more than I like colours.'

THIS PAGE Victoria's stunning vintage sideboard was just five dollars in a yard sale. 'I stripped off the white paint and sanded it down to reveal the bare wood,' she says. It's the perfect place for Victoria to display her favourite art prints, a large vintage 'V' and her impressive collection of sleek, teak candlesticks.

THIS PAGE A bespoke shelving unit provides plenty of storage and display space in the open-plan living room. Victoria arranges her books, artworks and ornaments in an orderly but relaxed fashion to avoid a cluttered look. Sheepskin rugs and cushions/pillows soften the appearance — and feel — of Victoria's on-trend wirework armchairs.

OPPOSITE Harlequin-style diamonds have been subtly incorporated into the living room scheme with a Moroccan-style rug, Ikat-print cushions/pillows and a stylish *Vogue* print for a cohesive look. 'I love this photo,' says Victoria. 'I like the way that everything is rushing past the model, who is calm and confident in the middle of all the action.'

She sums up her style succinctly as 'a mash-up of old and new.' In her dining area, she has a sideboard bought for five dollars in a yard sale 25 years ago but also a wooden pendant light by hip brand West Elm. In the living room, Victoria's 1960s teak coffee table, which was an Etsy vintage find, sits on a rug from high street giant Target.

Her home is filled with interesting objects and yet feels tidy and organised. 'The key to an uncluttered space is putting like objects together,' she confides. 'For example, I have a lot of books, but they are all stacked together and sorted by colour. I do have junk – but I hide it away! I had sliding doors put on my living room bookcase to conceal all the clutter and art supplies inside.'

There are personal treasures in this eclectic mix, too. Victoria's great-grandparents owned the Downie Brothers' Circus in the 1930s, so she has a black and white photograph showing its old advertising posters. 'I do feel as though I'm juggling most of the time, so perhaps the reason I'm fairly adept at it is that it's in my genes,' she laughs. Another precious print on display is a photo of her late father picking oranges. 'A friend coloured the oranges digitally for me and it's my favourite piece of wall art,' she says.

Although she spends her days at the forefront of cutting-edge design and technology, Victoria appreciates the simpler things in life. 'I love listening to my iPod but I also have a repro of a vintage Crosley record player and love the imperfect sound of an old Joni Mitchell vinyl on a Sunday afternoon,' she says. 'It's still nice to get up and change a record – there's something nostalgic about it.'

Similarly, she enjoys the peaceful ritual of making fresh coffee in the morning and is not averse to some good old-fashioned crafting from time to time. 'I sewed my dining chair seat cushion/ pillow covers from an old 1950s curtain/drape panel,' says Victoria. 'As long as you don't look too closely at them, they look great!'

OPPOSITE 'I'm always drawn to vintage blankets,' says Victoria. 'I like to mix pretty patterns together.' She keeps her favourites stacked on top of her wardrobe/closet and refreshes her bedroom's look whenever she fancies it by simply draping a different one on the bed.

TOP RIGHT Victoria's bentwood onion pendant light gives her dining room a retro look and blends in with her other wooden accessories and furniture. As it's exposed, Victoria has chosen an attractive vintage-style light bulb with a traditional filament.

BOTTOM RIGHT Only simple wooden and ceramic utensils, and pared-back tools can be found in Victoria's stylish kitchen. Black high-gloss worksurfaces prevent the look from slipping into 'rustic'. Despite the natural materials and raw elements, the overall look is fresh and modern.

Victoria loves:

- **Door Sixteen**, doorsixteen.com.
- **EmmasDesignBlog**, emmas.blogg.se.
- **DesignLoveFest**, designlovefest.com.
- **The Sartorialist**, thesartorialist.com.
- **Clementine**, clementinedaily.com.

SHOPS:
- **Papa Stour,** papastour.com. I like unique handmade items so enjoy exploring this Scottish design site.
- **Ferm Living,** fermliving.com. For inspiring patterns, colours and unexpected combinations.
- **Factory20,** factory20.com. Has amazing industrial vintage pieces to admire.

Top blogging tips:

- Blog about your passions. If people like your aesthetic, they'll follow you.
- Stay true to yourself – don't emulate other blogs – be natural. The more your blog reflects you, the better it is.
- A professional designer can make your blog look great. If you can't afford a designer, you could trade skills – if you're a good photographer or a great writer, you can help them in return for them helping you. I'm all in favour of a bit of bartering to get help. It's a good way to make things happen without having to spend a lot of money.

style tip

Rather than installing traditional kitchen lighting, fit mismatched, dainty, Victorian glass lampshades above kitchen worktops for a pretty look.

A stylish Smeg fridge, glass light fittings and rectangular 'metro' wall tiles bring retro style to the open-plan kitchen-diner at the rear of the house, which overlooks a pretty, flower-filled garden. Jill's collection of colourful tins fills open shelves in an alcove, while appliances are hidden away behind grey, folding doorfronts.

LEFT Mismatched chairs and seat cushions/pillows give the open-plan dining area a casual feel. The flooring in the kitchen was inherited from the previous owners but Jill stained it a darker colour. 'Now it has a sort of ship deck effect,' she says.

BELOW Dried Hydrangea heads from Jill's wedding bouquet create a Victorian-style display on the marble mantelpiece in the cosy reading room.

My Friend's House

myfriendshouse.co.uk

Design journalist and blogger Jill Macnair lives in a three-storey Victorian house in a leafy corner of East Dulwich, south London, with her husband, Neil, and two young children, Rafer and Gilda. Her home has bags of character and a quintessentially British feel thanks to a heady mix of mid-century modern furniture and a bevy of secondhand buys. It's clear that Jill has an instinctive knack for decorating her home beautifully and an innate talent for cherry-picking antiques and blending them with cutting-edge designer buys. Jill's good friend and co-blogger, Ros Anderson, lives nearby and often pops round for a cup of tea.

Friends Jill and Ros describe their quirky online realm as 'light-hearted and a little bit ramshackle', which sums it up well. It's a refreshingly witty and dry take on the world of interiors, filled with design news, amusing anecdotes and serendipitous nuggets. 'Our readers always like personal posts the best,' says Jill. 'I once blogged about how my dad came to stay and helpfully fixed lots of things around our house with black tape. For example, the drawer inside our Smeg fridge. It was very practical, but he didn't care about how it looked at all.'

'I wanted a drawer unit like this for ages and finally found this one in an architectural salvage shop in Glasgow.'

THIS PAGE Blue Delphiniums fill a glass chemistry flask used as a vase on Jill's bedroom drawer unit. Jill has a knack of placing modern accessories with antique finds to create a home that's beautiful and unique. Her impeccably good taste shines through in every room.

LEFT 'I like odd shelves in unexpected places such as above doors or low down at skirting board level,' says Jill. The contemporary lightbox on the wall inside the alcove is from Lilly's Lightbox Company. Mid-century modern style sofas with tapered beech legs give the room a 1950s flavour.

OPPOSITE The cosy reading room is home to Jill's music collection, a family photograph gallery and a pair of handsome Art Deco armchairs. This room oozes Victorian grandeur with dark walls, an ornate marble fireplace and luxurious floor-to-ceiling curtains/drapes made from Florence Broadhurst fabric. Jill has painted the skirting boards dark to match the walls for theatrical colour saturation.

The duo regularly poke fun at themselves and one another and have, as a result, built up a legion of readers who welcome their alternative approach. The two London-based bloggers don't attempt to pretend that everything in their homes is perfect – but that's all part of their charm. In fact, Ros once posted a photo of her window box filled with dead, dried up plants and refers to her mischievous cat as 'the anti-stylist'.

'It was Ros's idea to start a blog,' says Jill. 'I'd had nine months off work to have my son and it was a good way to get back into the habit of writing regularly. Blogging together means we can have a conversation online, which gives both the blog and our friendship an extra dimension. Blogging has carried our relationship forward as well as cementing my passion for design.'

Although Jill says the blog doesn't influence her home directly, she does feel that it motivates her to put creative ideas into action. 'If I talk about something on such a public forum, it encourages me to actually do it!'

The friends often share their love of vintage homewares on their blog, giving readers glimpses of their rich pickings from local junk shops. One of Jill's most

ABOVE The bird mobile in Jill's daughter's bedroom was made using a kit designed by artist Alice Melvin for the Tate Gallery.

RIGHT In Jill's bedroom, vintage floral bedlinen from British companies such as Liberty of London and Toast has been mixed together with linen accessories from Merci in Paris. The blanket is by British textile designer Eleanor Pritchard.

treasured possessions is her impressive 20-drawer wooden storage unit, originally reclaimed from a shop and now used as a dresser for clothes in her bedroom. 'I love the cup handles and the glass top,' says Jill. 'I wanted one for ages. It's a useful display area and adds an element of imperfection. I don't like things to be too slick and shiny.'

Elsewhere in the bedroom, more evidence of Jill's roving magpie eye can be seen; a trio of dark earthenware bottles perch on a tallboy unit, elegant sepia photographs lean on the mantelpiece and a vintage marmalade jar is filled with pretty Peonies.

Although Jill loves designer buys and retro finds, she's also good at sniffing out high street bargains. 'My gorgeous rug came from IKEA,' she says. 'It was such good value for money and the perfect grey colour.' The windows have simple black-out roller blinds/shades instead of curtains/drapes, giving the room a clean, contemporary feel.

Jill is an expert at creating inviting spaces. Downstairs, the elegant, airy living room leads through to a dark reading room, complete with curvaceous Art Deco German armchairs and a mid-century modern hostess trolley that

THIS PAGE Jill's daughter's bedroom has a cheery, yellow wardrobe/closet and Ercol chair with original fabric. Victorian tiles create a colourful hearth in front of the period fireplace and floorboards are painted white for a clean, airy feel. The curtains/drapes are made from ditsy, floral print fabric purchased at Kingdom Interiors.

LEFT Upstairs, in a converted attic, Jill has created a cosy corner for blogging. She bought the Danish desk in a local antiques shop and found the 1950s French classroom map online. 'Neil's father is from Bethlehem, so the map of Palestine is really personal to us,' she says. An Anglepoise desk lamp completes the vintage workspace look.

OPPOSITE, TOP LEFT By sorting her books according to colour, Jill has turned an old bookcase into an eye catching focal point in her office.

OPPOSITE, TOP RIGHT Jewellery is stored on a colourful ceramic plate from Swedish design house Marimekko, which looks particularly striking on Jill's bright red side table.

OPPOSITE, BOTTOM LEFT Jill's bathroom walls are wallpapered. 'We didn't coat the wallpaper with anything and so far it's not peeled off!' she chuckles.

serves as a cocktail bar. 'We painted the walls in Farrow & Ball's Castle Gray – a deep grey-green that contrasts dramatically with the white walls in the next room,' reveals Jill. 'I keep my music collection in here and it's a great space to unwind in.'

When it comes to her home, Jill can be very particular – and her attention to detail always pays off. 'For the kitchen, I wanted mustard yellow metro wall tiles but couldn't find the perfect colour anywhere,' she says. 'I ended up ordering them online from Heath Ceramics

in San Francisco... they're exactly what I was after.' In the living room, she fixed a single floating shelf low down in an alcove, while, on a chimney breast in the reading room, a round mirror is bravely positioned off-centre. She's nailed the art of imperfection, perfectly.

It might look stunning, but Jill's home is still a work in progress. 'I'm obsessed with re-doing our bedroom at the moment. I'm really into a pale, blush pink colour and I'd also like to re-upholster some chairs,' she says, already planning her next project.

OPPOSITE A statement retro sideboard in Joy's bedroom is covered with colourful accessories and trinkets. 'If I don't keep things out, I forget I have them and never wear them,' explains Joy. 'I can't wear every single hair accessory or pretty necklace I own every day, so by displaying them I get to appreciate them.'

RIGHT Joy's bedside lamps are made of marble and brass; 'two materials that always look really good together,' says Joy.

BELOW RIGHT 'I love modern textiles and designs but I mix new pieces with vintage and found objects to add character to my home,' says Joy.

Oh Joy!

ohjoy.blogs.com

Full-time blogger and designer Joy Cho lives with her husband, Bob, and daughter, Ruby, in a spacious three-bedroom apartment, on top of a hill in the Silver Lake neighbourhood of Los Angeles. The height, coupled with superb views of the city skyline, gives Joy's home a feeling of freedom. Her style is smart, sassy and polished. She's combined sleek mid-century pieces of furniture with modern American accessories for dramatic results and has recently child-proofed her home, discreetly and cleverly, so her young daughter can enjoy the space, too.

'We moved here in 2010,' says Joy. 'Both my husband and I loved the location and the incredible views over the city. Our street is conveniently close to some great shops and restaurants but it's super-quiet, too.' It's also just ten minutes away from her new Hollywood studio,

a light-filled 'grown-up candyland', where colourful furniture and accessories surround Joy and her colleagues. She used to work from home but now needs a bigger space to house her thriving creative businesses. Formerly a graphic designer for fashion brands, Joy went on to

ABOVE Fresh blooms fill a sunny, yellow vase on Joy's dining table. Brightly-coloured placemats beneath the vase complete the cheery, contemporary look.

ABOVE RIGHT Gold accessories give Joy's living room a luxurious feel. 'Our main living space is the perfect blend of Bob's style and my style,' says Joy. 'We had two makeovers – one masculine, one feminine – then merged our favourite elements from each.'

OPPOSITE 'Wallpapering all the walls in a big room is a bold move and not something I would have ever thought to do alone,' admits Joy. 'I love the effect, though – it's a great base for our furniture and accessories.'

design home accessories and textiles before launching her own studio in 2005. Since then, she's worked on everything from stationery and children's clothing to wallpaper and a wireless computer mouse, has authored books about creativity and blogging, and also offers consultation services to brands.

She's busy indeed, but her calm, ordered home offers a clue to the secret of her success. Somehow, despite the baby, the cats and the hectic career, the apartment is immaculate. This is a woman who is incredibly organised and focused. She's also good at collaborating. Interior designer and stylist Emily Henderson worked on Joy's new studio interior, and also decorated Joy's living and dining room areas at home as part of a TV makeover.

The walls are covered with gold and white Petal Pusher paper, designed by Joy, while the rest of the large room is filled with smart, teak furniture and metallic gold and navy blue accessories. The overall effect is gorgeously glamorous – a stunning backdrop which Joy likes to constantly update as her tastes evolve. 'As a blogger, I am always seeing inspiring things,' she says.

'I'm constantly updating my home with new accessories and smaller details to freshen things up. At the moment, I'm obsessed with my constantly growing collection of vases and vessels for flowers!'

Joy's home is, unsurprisingly, a hub of creativity. The walls of the living room and dining area act as mini galleries, showcasing carefully-arranged art prints and illustrations by friends and fellow designers, while adhesive, metallic pink polka dots decorate the walls and doors of her home office. In her bedroom, Joy has turned storage into a feature by fixing vintage wooden hangers to the wall and using them to display her favourite pieces of jewellery.

Pattern is something she is clearly passionate about. Her rugs, bedlinen, curtains/drapes and cushions/pillows are

PREVIOUS PAGE Joy has placed a console table behind her sofa, which is a handy place for ornaments – it almost serves the same purpose as a mantelpiece. Artworks have been carefully arranged above in a symmetrical formation that avoids looking too formal. A strong navy and gold theme runs throughout the scheme.

LEFT 'We used to have a glass dining table with a chrome base,' says Joy. 'It was lovely but not particularly safe for Ruby, so we swapped it for a more sturdy wooden table. As I get older, I value quality more. I invest in key pieces that will stand the test of time, then refresh my look with more affordable accessories.'

ABOVE Alphabet fridge magnets provide a fun way to leave messages in the kitchen. Ruby's toys haven't been banished to a bedroom; instead, her play area has been incorporated into the main living room, where she has her own art table and storage baskets for toys.

THIS PAGE Plush blue velvet curtains/drapes hang on a brass rail, creating a luxurious look and linking the open-plan living and dining room spaces together. Eames chairs bring a modern twist to the space.

OPPOSITE, ABOVE LEFT
One of Joy's cats lounges on the bed, which is currently draped with patterned textiles in yellow and orange, but gets a mini makeover regularly. A linen cupboard/closet on the landing is used to store Joy's impressive collection of patterned bedlinen.

OPPOSITE, ABOVE RIGHT
From fun snaps of a family holiday in France to her popular Hers & Mine series (where she compares an item she owns or wears to something similar belonging to her daughter), Joy shares a lot of her life with her readers.

ABOVE The walls of Joy's spacious home office are decorated with pink foil polka dots. They bring a feminine touch to the room and provide a fun backdrop to a pair of white, floating shelves, where Joy displays treasures and trinkets. 'Now that I have a separate studio to work in, my home office is less frequently used,' she says.

OPPOSITE, BELOW LEFT
A row of wooden hangers fixed to Joy's bedroom wall is home to her jewellery collection. From on-trend geometric necklaces in pastel hues to cute candy-coloured pom-pom hairclips, her signature style is fresh and girly, with plenty of hot pink.

a medley of contrasting zig zags, stripes, trellis-effect geometrics and tribal-inspired prints. It could easily be too much, but she's expertly kept the colour palette harmonious throughout so it all gels neatly together.

Her home is pretty, but practical, too. The recent arrival of Joy's daughter Ruby triggered a baby-proofing makeover, so the pristine white sofa now has a washable, blue slipcover on the seats, soft, Moroccan-style pouffes have replaced a sharp-cornered coffee table and a natty storage cabinet now houses glassware and Bob's whiskey collection. The adaptations are subtle – proof that a child-friendly home can be stylish as well as safe.

When Joy launched her blog back in 2005, the blogging scene was just getting started. 'Blogs weren't popular in the way that they are now,' she explains. 'I started

mine because I wanted a place to keep my inspirations at a time when I had a lot of transition. The site slowly became more popular and it helped me to launch my own design studio.'

Joy often shares photos of her cute daughter, Ruby, and says her readers always respond to the more personal posts she publishes; 'people love authenticity and seeing what I do in my real life and with my family,' she says.

Her cheery name suits her perfectly and she feels lucky that her working life brings her such pleasure. 'Blogging has created a job I never thought I'd have and didn't even think was possible,' she says. 'It allows me to explore so many various, fulfilling creative outlets and it's become an amazing way to share the things I love with others.'

Joy loves:

- **Typepad**, typepad.com. The platform I host my blog on.
- **Designlovefest**, designlovefest.com.
- **Taza**, lovetaza.com.

SHOPS:

- **Leif,** leifshop.com. A great assortment of beautiful gifts from homeware to jewellery
- **Mini Rodini,** minirodini.com. For the cutest and slightly edgy kids' clothing.
- **J.Crew,** jcrew.com. Classic, modern and feminine clothing I can wear year-round.

Top blogging tips:

- Do your research. Since there are so many blogs these days, it's important to make sure you're doing something that's different and not too similar to what's already out there, both in subject matter and aesthetic.
- Be genuine. Write about the things that you really love and are excited to write about every day.

homespun

OPPOSITE Jane's spacious dining room is flooded with light thanks to large windows and white walls. By removing the wall that separated the living room and dining room, Jane has created an airy, open-plan space. Instead of trying to disguise unsightly pipes beneath the radiator, she has turned them into a mini feature by wrapping them with brightly-coloured masking tape.

LEFT 'I painted the dining room wall but left a white border, so it's like a frame,' explains Jane. 'I like the way it turns the wall into a sort of backdrop for displaying things in front of. I often use the corner as a place to take photographs for my shop and blog.'

BELOW LEFT A vintage oil painting, wooden vases, a pretty plate and a delicate branch are expertly arranged on Jane's living room sideboard.

All The Luck In The World

blog.alltheluckintheworld.nl

Blogger and boutique owner Jane Schouten is a talented hunter-gatherer with a magpie eye for treasure, but takes little credit for her carefully-curated collections. 'They are all unintentional,' she says modestly, preferring instead to claim that her skill for sifting the wheat from the chaff in thrift stores and at flea markets is sheer luck. Despite the name of her blog and her humble protestations, it is Jane's eye for spotting the unusual and the interesting combined with her innate ability to bring unexpected elements together, apparently effortlessly, that has given her cosy home a look that is inspiring – and all her own.

Jane's 1950s home in Rhenen is an eclectic mix of the kitsch, colourful and creative. It is a vintage paradise; cupboards are filled to the brim with pile upon pile of textiles, rows of Virgin Mary ornaments cluster on ledges and mantelpieces, colourful rattan furniture sits alongside

sleek 1960s sofas and every wall and surface displays something fascinating to explore and admire.

'I run a store selling vintage furniture and contemporary home accessories with my daughter, Nina, who's a goldsmith. Both my daughters – Nina and Robin – live in

style tip

Link two separate spaces by using the same flooring and painting walls in both sections the same colour for a fluid, cohesive feel.

ABOVE A row of small, brass, stag-shaped hooks in the dining room provides a place for Jane to hang a chain of family photo frames, jewellery and her favourite vintage bags.

LEFT Jane has painted her vintage kitchen cabinets pink inside, to set off her hoard of colourful coffee cups and tableware. From psychedelic floral designs to pastel-coloured milk glass pieces, she's amassed a huge selection.

Amsterdam, but I prefer to live down here, where it's quieter. I have nice neighbours and the thrift stores are cheaper!' says Jane.

Some of the treasures in Jane's home are stock for her shop, either on the way to be sold or that she can't bear to part with. 'I get attached,' she explains with a shrug. 'The light fitting above my dining table was in my attic for four years. I always intended to sell it, so I got it down one day – just to check that it worked – hung it up, and it's still there now. It looks good. Maybe it will stay there. Maybe it won't.'

Jane talks about her home as if it is a happy accident, where furniture and objects come and go like the tides – a place where she observes the transience and flux but does not get involved. This could not be further from the truth. If the contents of her home is an orchestra, then Jane is the conductor – albeit a humble one.

'I stopped collecting birds, but somehow, they keep finding me,' she muses, gesturing to stacks of delicate bird tapestries and rows of pretty tumblers painted with finches and bluebirds.

THIS PAGE 'The wallpaper on my kitchen wall is probably from the 1960s. I found it in a vintage shop in Amsterdam,' says Jane. A narrow shelf provides a perch for her latest flock of birdy buys and a beautiful tea tin.

'Almost everything I own is secondhand,' she adds. But her look is far from old-fashioned – contemporary additions are mixed in, too; a laboratory flask with a hot pink base here, a fluorescent blanket by a cutting-edge Dutch textile designer there. 'I like to mix old with new,' explains Jane. 'I have no rules. I just like what I like.'

THIS PAGE By keeping the fundamental elements of her living room — such as walls, curtains/drapes and flooring — simple and plain, Jane is able to have fun mixing colourful accessories. 1960s furniture works well with retro rattan pieces and second-hand finds to create a chic eclectic mix.

Jane's a skilled seamstress, so makes her own curtains/drapes and cushion/pillow covers upstairs in her quirky craft room, which is filled with supplies, equipment and precious possessions. Stacks of old medicine cabinets provide useful storage space and Jane's trademark first-aid-style cross sign can be seen everywhere.

THIS PAGE 'This cabinet is in my living room at the moment because the shop is full,' says Jane. 'I often keep a piece of furniture at home for a while to decide how I'm going to display it in the shop, then when I finally take it to the shop, I display it in a completely different way anyway!'

THIS PAGE   The contemporary blanket on Jane's sofa is by Dutch textile artist Mae Engelgeer. 'We sell these in our shop and I like the contrast between the dark and fluorescent colours,' says Jane. A group of Virgin Mary figurines and a 1960s swan print create a kitsch display on the mantelpiece.

OPPOSITE   Jane's craft room is filled with precious vintage plunder, from tiny cameo portraits in gilt frames to ornate curtains/drapes. The Singer sewing machine was picked up at a secondhand shop. 'It still works perfectly,' says thrifty Jane, who sews many of her own accessories and enjoys making good luck charms for her customers.

LEFT In Jane's office, a pretty lace curtain/drape conceals clutter and an old painted picture frame serves as a pin board for inspirational photos and postcards. 'I sewed the seat cushion/pillow from a piece of vintage fabric – a lucky find,' says Jane.

BELOW 'I found these old drawers in France and really liked the faded vintage paper labels on them, so just left them in place,' says Jane.

'The cross logo is my shop's sign, so it's my signature symbol now, too,' says Jane. 'I've always collected crosses, long before the shop. To me, a cross is a sign of positivity. It's a plus sign.' Little crosses made from washi tape adorn the walls and, once you start looking, the symbol can be spotted in almost every room; a pink cross magnet is stuck to a metal box in the kitchen, a turquoise, glittery cross hangs beside the fireplace in the living room.

Jane's aesthetic is refreshingly unfussy and relaxed. She has mastered the ancient art of *wabi-sabi* – of discovering beauty in imperfection. 'I found my old rattan rocking chair half-painted and I like it that way,' she says. 'It's half white and half bare. I love it so much that I can't take it to the shop – it's become my favourite place to sit.' Her approach is that of a rescuer, adopting unloved pieces and giving them the attention she feels they deserve.

THIS PAGE Painted boxes, glass-fronted display cases and medicine cabinets are stacked together artfully in the craft room, providing nooks and crannies for Jane to fill with her handmade creations and flea market finds.

ALS IK EEN GROENENDE TWYG
IN MYN HART BEWAAR,
ZAL DE ZANGVOGEL ZEKER KOMEN...

ABOVE Upstairs, cupboards are filled to bursting point with wooden embroidery hoops, old glass jars, paintbrushes and lengths of sparkling beaded ribbon – ingredients for Jane's many ongoing projects. 'I have loads of tapestries,' she chuckles. 'I still have plans to make something with all of them one day. I'm not sure what yet – but one day I'll need them.'

Jane's house is filled with memories, mementos and warmth. Family photographs, keepsakes and souvenirs can be found in every room, making it the polar opposite of a perfect set or glossy show room – it tells her story and has real character.

Jane's home inspires most of her blog content, which is largely visual and often consists of styled photos that she takes around the house. 'I try to record what I'm doing but I don't always get around to it,' she admits. 'I only post when I feel like it and I use my blog as a place to share my photos and inspirations,' she adds. 'I've met some amazing people through blogging who I would never have met otherwise. It makes the world feel like quite a small place.'

OPPOSITE, TOP LEFT In her bedroom, Jane has cleverly hidden her TV inside a white-painted antique cabinet. 'The crocheted blanket is a vintage find I picked up years ago,' Jane explains.

OPPOSITE, TOP RIGHT Jane's original creations combine old-fashioned techniques with cutting-edge craft for exciting results. 'I love using embroidery hoops as frames,' says Jane.

OPPOSITE, BOTTOM LEFT Quirky vignettes fill every corner of Jane's cosy home. She has natural flair for bringing together unexpected objects – a glittery blue faux coral fan, a battered first aid tin, a glass chemistry flask – to create a fresh new look.

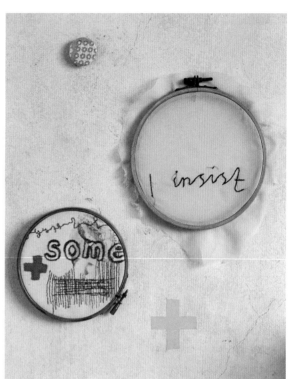

Jane loves:

- Other bloggers. Many of them are now my friends.
- **Facebook**, facebook.com.

SHOPS:

- **Mae Engelgeer,** mae-engelgeer.nl.
- **Een Nieuw Avontuur,** eennieuwavontuur.com.
- **Etsy**, etsy.com.

Top blogging tips:

- Don't start writing every day or your readers will expect it. Start by posting once a week so you can keep it up.
- Try to develop your photography skills as good images can make your blog stand out.
- I host my blog on Wordpress, which I chose because I thought it would give me more design options but it's not the easiest to use! I'm not good at the technical back-end stuff. I can post, but I'm not great at extras.
- Bookmarking — I just bookmark my favourite blogs and read them every now and again.

Ida Interior Lifestyle

idainteriorlifestyle.com

It was just eighteen months ago that interior stylist and freelance photographer Ilaria Chiaratti and her husband, Alberto, moved into their spacious 1920s Eindhoven home. A talented crafter – who spends her free time crocheting, up-cycling furniture, sewing and stitching – Ilaria has, in a very short time, put her own stamp on the airy Dutch building. Her secret? Mixing vintage pieces with her own creations and personalising every corner of the house with fun embellishments, from paper bunting to polka dot wall stickers. Add into the mix a courtyard garden draped with twinkling pea light garlands, a curious kitten called Penny Lane and three floors of colourful interiors to explore and the adventure begins.

'We are originally from Milan in Italy, where life was stressful and fast-paced,' says Ilaria, in her chirpy, upbeat voice. 'But here in the Netherlands, it's totally different. Everything is slower and people are much more laid back. It suits us.'

It was the light and space that first attracted Ilaria to her Eindhoven home. 'I wanted an older building with character, big windows and a room that could become a studio,' she explains.

ABOVE Ilaria has given her laundry room a mini makeover, transforming it from a drab, dated space into a fun, colourful room. She's covered unsightly appliances with pink curtains/drapes, wallpapered old cupboard doors and laid a cheerful rug on the floor.

RIGHT The oak dresser in the dining room has been given an Ilaria Chiaratti twist with patterned ceramic handles/ knobs. She's personalised it further with fun whimsical phrases, written directly onto the glass panes using a white marker pen.

THIS PAGE 'The living room is big but it still feels cosy,' says Ilaria, who has divided the living and dining areas in her open-plan space using rugs and lighting. The chimney breast has been covered with tiny polka dot wall stickers for a playful feature. 'I love the combination of turquoise blue and hot pink,' she says.

TEA FOR TWO
AND
TWO FOR TEA

'I'm always drawn to an all-white background, warm teak furniture and layers of colourful, hand-crafted accessories.'

THIS PAGE Ilaria's living room is a relaxed space, filled with high street bargains, stylish second-hand furniture and homemade crocheted accessories. 'My coffee table was just a few euros at a flea market,' reveals Ilaria. 'The legs are original and the top is newer, but the shape is nice and you can't tell, so I don't care!' The floors are made of warm, solid oak. 'I like natural wood,' she says. 'The gorgeous floors in this house were one of the reasons we fell in love with it in the first place.'

ABOVE 'I collect wool in a glass cabinet,' says Ilaria. 'I've always collected craft equipment. When I was 14, I studied graphic design in Italy, so gathered a lot of pencils and crayons. I've had the stuff ever since. I always have the right tools at my fingertips.'

RIGHT Illaria's impressive stash of colourful Japanese Washi masking tape lets her create temporary displays whenever she fancies. At the moment, she is using the tape to frame panels on her craft room door (see above left), turning something plain into a unique feature that reflects her bubbly personality.

ABOVE RIGHT Ilaria made her computer screen cover from an old tote bag. 'I like the motto: "Today isn't just another day. Today I'll create something new." It's a good thing to read every morning before I start work!' Her studio is situated in a converted loft space with plenty of natural daylight — essential for crafting.

THIS PAGE There are neat stacks of crocheted squares and big baskets bulging with balls of wool all around Ilaria's creative home. 'It's always nice to have the right wool for the right project,' she laughs. On her blog, Ilaria shares fun mottoes such as 'Behind every great crocheter is a huge pile of yarn' and 'The more you crochet, the warmer you get.'

'This place was perfect as it had a huge attic I could work in, plenty of period features and bags of charm. We haven't looked back.'

With high ceilings, wooden floorboards, an original fireplace and large rooms, it has all the ingredients of a stylish home, but it's Ilaria's passion for pattern and her superior crafting skills that make this interior stand out. 'My great aunt taught me how to crochet over ten years ago,' says Ilaria. 'I started by making small items such as scarves, but these days I'm into making blankets and cushion/pillow covers for our home.' Ilaria's colourful crocheted creations are all around.

If you look closely, there are light-hearted, personalised details to be found, too – this is a home where informality and humour are embraced. On the glass of her dining room cabinet, Ilaria has written the phrase 'tea for two and two for tea' in front of her collection of pretty, vintage teacups. 'I use a white pen that writes on glass,' she explains. 'In the winter, I decorate the window that faces the street with festive phrases and decorations and we get a lot of compliments from our neighbours!'

Ilaria says she is constantly 'experimenting with little displays' around the house. 'An Italian designer sent me some little wooden decorations for Christmas but I liked

LEFT 'Our bed is made from reclaimed wood,' says Ilaria. 'Finding the right bed was a real struggle until I found Jorg Steigerhout, a company that sells furniture made from recycled wood, based in Amsterdam. It's solid and quite unusual.' The chunky headboard is a handy place to prop prints and homemade decorations.

ABOVE Dainty handmade wooden Christmas tree decorations by designer Katia di Maglie adorn the wall of Ilaria's guest bedroom, creating a year-round festive display.

them so much I wanted to display them all year round, so I just taped them onto the wall,' chuckles Ilaria. 'I have a lot of fun with Washi tape. My house is not a *fait accompli* – it's constantly changing and evolving every day.'

The chimney breast in the living room is peppered with polka dots, delicate doilies are taped to the walls as pieces of art and even the doors of Ilaria's studio are decorated with strips of tape in a rainbow of colours. Ilaria is an expert at layering. 'As long as you get the balance right and don't over-do it, it's fine. Start with a blank canvas – white walls, or a plain sofa – then introduce patterned accessories that feature colours from a single palette.'

Many of Ilaria's favourite possessions were picked up for next to nothing at markets. Her 1960s, teak coffee table was just three euros, her vintage typewriter 'around seven' – she's a thrifty bargain hunter.

Her make-do-and-mend approach has enabled her to transform a drab utility room into a beautiful space. 'When we moved in, it was dark and depressing,' she says. 'I needed a temporary solution to prettify it until we can update it properly, so I've wallpapered all the cupboard doors, covered the appliances with fuchsia pink curtains/drapes, put down a colourful rug and painted the walls with bright turquoise paint.'

THIS PAGE From the rug and lampshade to the bunting and cushion/pillow covers, there's a stunning array of crocheted accessories in Ilaria's welcoming guest bedroom. Her creations are so popular that she's opened the IDA Yarn Shop online and now sells her handiwork to an army of fans.

Elsewhere, other areas have also been given the Ilaria treatment; a chest of drawers/dresser in the attic has been revived with a coat of fresh, coral paint and a set of new drawer handles/knobs, an old tote bag has been refashioned into a chic computer screen cover and little words – made from wool and wire – perch hither and thither, turning otherwise empty nooks and crannies into mini focal points.

In the hallway, Ilaria has made the outline of a house on the wall using Washi tape and fixed a sheet of paper inside it. 'Take a smile…' it instructs, above a row of tear-off pieces of paper with hand-drawn smiling faces to take away. What with all the colour and craft – not to mention the cute kitten – by the time guests leave Ilaria's home, they will already be beaming from ear-to-ear anyway.

ABOVE Floating, blue, open shelves in the kitchen are home to Ilaria's joyful medley of decorative tableware. There are plenty of pieces here from Dutch design brands, such as PiP Studio.

OPPOSITE, BOTTOM LEFT Ilaria makes her signature *mots au crochet* using coloured wool and wire to sell in her online shop. The laid-back, handwritten-effect lettering is popular with buyers and other bloggers.

OPPOSITE, TOP RIGHT 'It's important to customize even the smallest of spaces,' says Ilaria, who has turned a simple shelf in her hallway into a stylish display area by framing it with Washi tape in a welcoming house shape.

OPPOSITE, BOTTOM RIGHT Ilaria has decorated a mini wooden drawer unit from IKEA using fun stickers and the same coral paint she used to paint her bigger chest of drawers/dresser beneath.

Illaria loves:

Yvestown, yvestown.com.
Wood Wool Stool, woodwoolstool.blogspot.nl.
Fjeldborg, blog.fjeldborg.no.
Byfryd, byfryd.com.
Appuntidi Casa, appuntidicasa.com.
Latazzina Blu, latazzinablu.blogspot.nl.

SHOPS:
- **Snug Studio,** etsy.com/uk/shop/snugstudio.
- **Camp Cirrus,** etsy.com/shop/campcirrus.
- **La Cerise Sur Le Gateau,** shop.lacerisesurlegateau.fr/en.
- **Nina Invorm,** etsy.com/shop/Ninainvorm.

Top blogging tips:

- Take care with the design of your blog — it's your online business card. Keep it simple and divide sections into pages.
- To build up an audience, create connections with other bloggers. Be open and comment on other blogs that you enjoy and organically your network will grow and develop.

colour fun

LEFT A vintage sideboard in Jonathan's dining area provides a showcase space for him to display his collection of mid-century modern ceramics. 'I'm like a bower bird — I'm always drawn to teal blue and shiny things,' says Jonathan. The brass starburst mirror on the wall above was picked up at an estate sale.

BELOW LEFT Jonathan's terracotta, geo planter pot is by MGMY Studio — he bought it on Etsy. It blends in well with the orange and blue scheme in his living room.

Happy Mundane

happymundane.com

Graphic designer and blogger Jonathan Lo lives in a two-bedroom house in Orange County, southern California, with his dog, Pepé. His confident use of colour makes his home a cheery, bright space — a reflection of his sunny, happy-go-lucky personality. Eclectic and playful, his look is a heady mix of mid-century modern finds, clever DIY makes, contemporary designer pieces and influences as diverse as tropical, Hawaiian style and sleek, urban hotel chic. Refusing to subscribe to any one style, Jonathan's managed to combine all his various passions to create a stunning, unique interior that's filled with fun features.

Jonathan's dining area demonstrates his ability to pick and mix various elements from very different looks and blend them together flawlessly to create a scheme that's his own. The chairs are all different – colonial-inspired, teal bentwood, mid-century teak and a smart black seat.

'I appreciate such a wide range of styles, it's hard for me to just stick with one thing,' explains Jonathan, who runs his own graphic design business and blogs about interiors in his free time. 'As long as there's something that unites the various elements, you can mix and match. In

THIS PAGE Jonathan's open-plan living space has a border made of panels of retro textured wallpaper at dado level. 'Your eye follows the panels around the room – it visually unifies the space but also designates separate zones,' says Jonathan. 'I like introducing colour and texture in small portions here and there.'

my dining area, the table is the constant, so the mismatched chairs look good together. Similarly, in my guest bedroom, I've chosen a white sofa so that I can introduce lots of different multi-coloured cushions/pillows without worrying about the overall look – it just works.'

His light-filled home, set on a quiet street in Orange County, California, has an unusual split-level layout – but that's one of the many features that first attracted Jonathan to the building. 'It's so light,' he says, happily. 'The inside feels very much like a San Francisco duplex – you enter in the middle of the house, then you can either go upstairs or downstairs. I like the open-plan living area, too. It's airy and spacious.'

Jonathan has introduced panels of colour and texture to the walls in order to separate the open space into clearly defined dining and living areas. Retro, wood-chip-style papered sections, cork and mirror tiles and painted areas, all at dado level, form a flowing border around the plain, white-washed walls that give the illusion of separate yet unified spaces. 'It leads the eye around the room,' says Jonathan. The mirrored panel is reminiscent of a 1960s hatch/window to another room.

'I like using colour to create little nooks – it's just a splash but it creates such a cosy corner.'

OPPOSITE Jonathan's dog, Pepé, snuggles up on his favourite chair in the guest bedroom, where Jonathan has painted a portion of the wall and ceiling in bright tangerine to give the corner a strong identity. 'Paint is just temporary,' Jonathan points out. 'It's an easy way to divide up a space without actually building a wall!'

THIS PAGE Jonathan's living room is a heady 1970s-style mix of navy blue, teal and orange. 'The coffee table was an estate sale find,' reveals Jonathan. 'It's not my usual style but it's so elegant, I had to have it – even though I can barely lift it! It adds a bit of gravitas to my scheme – it's interesting how one piece can send you in another direction.'

LEFT By mixing vintage furniture with new, designer buys and some clever DIY creations, Jonathan's achieved a unique, chic and sleek interior. He painted the two artworks himself using his favourite colours because he couldn't find exactly what he wanted in any shops. Thanks to his design skills and intuitive use of colour, the result is expensive-looking, bespoke art that certainly doesn't look homemade.

BELOW A painted panel frames a floating display shelf in Jonathan's bedroom, where he has an ever-changing arrangement, currently featuring mini dolls' house furniture from IKEA, retro robots and 3D origami paper shapes.

In his bedroom, Jonathan employed a similar technique; small painted sections of the walls create mini focal points. 'As a graphic designer, I love to colour-block. I didn't want to paint a whole wall, it's too much of a commitment. I'm also really lazy, so smaller painted sections suit me.' On one wall, a pale blue panel provides an unfussy backdrop for a simple floating shelf. 'I like to frame my displays,' says Jonathan. 'The shelf is just from IKEA but, thanks to the blue frame, it's like a little art installation now.'

Jonathan's used his creative skills elsewhere in the bedroom, too, to create a high-end, boutique hotel look. 'I was inspired by a stay at the W Hotel in New York,' he reveals. 'The room I stayed in had a really high headboard with amazing impact. I wanted a similar look, but to buy a headboard that big would be really expensive and quite difficult to get into my house.' Undeterred, he bought a pair of doors at his local hardware shop, stained them teak, screwed them together, then fixed them to the wall with Velcro. 'It was so easy and only cost me about $200.'

THIS PAGE Jonathan's homemade headboard is a real triumph, lending his room an urban hotel look. Glossy, glass bedside tables/nightstands, geometric accessories and on-trend art prints complete the look. 'The colourful triangles cushion/pillow is by British textile artist Tamasyn Gambell,' he says. His bedroom is smart but deliberately not symmetrical – he is an expert at merging graphic shapes, panels of colour and patterned elements for a multi-layered scheme.

OPPOSITE, TOP RIGHT
Jonathan's passion for vintage accessories means he is constantly collecting. 'I have a garage full of antiques,' he confesses. 'When I drive to Palm Springs, I always take a long route so I can pop into all the thrift stores in the small towns along the way!'

OPPOSITE, TOP LEFT
Fashioned from wooden embroidery hoops and lengths of dowelling, Jonathan's graphic 1960s-style room divider looks like a pricey bespoke commission. Carefully-selected, eclectic art covers the hall wall behind, where pieces by contemporary artists are displayed with vintage finds.

Even the artwork on his bedroom walls is homemade. 'Most of my DIY projects come about because I can't find exactly what I'm looking for,' he explains. 'I painted the art canvases myself because I wanted them to go well with the colours in the cushions/pillows on my bed, and to have a kind of 1980s, post-modern, Memphis-style look... They're not complicated – I just used masking tape and painted some shapes.'

He speaks about his stunning, homemade room divider screen with similar modesty. 'I was inspired by a metal window grille I saw in Los Angeles, so just glued a load of embroidery hoops and dowelling together,' he recalls. 'It was a much bigger task than I thought it would be. I originally planned to do a whole wall, but could only manage four rows in the end,' he laughs. 'It looks fine but it's not very stable!' Unsurprisingly, Jonathan's posts about his DIY home décor projects are always among the most popular on his ever-growing blog.

On combining his work and blogging Jonathan notes, 'I had my graphic design and marketing business long before I started blogging... Because I have a lot of corporate clients, I originally wanted to keep my personal blog separate from work, but now I have a bigger following I'm trying to figure out a way to blend the two somehow.'

ABOVE With the Californian sunshine streaming in through the windows and a joyful celebration of colour at every turn, Jonathan's home is the embodiment of what ceramicist Jonathan Adler refers to as 'happy chic'. The smiling face vase is by Atelier Stella.

OPPOSITE, BOTTOM RIGHT A floral beaded curtain/drape provides a fun tropical touch in Jonathan's guest bedroom, which has a relaxed, holiday vibe.

Jonathan loves:

- **Bright Bazaar**, brightbazaarblog.com.
- **Design Sponge**, designsponge.com.
- **Poppytalk**, poppytalk.com.
- **Old Brand New**, oldbrandnewblog.com.
- **Jennifer Chong**, blog.jchongstudio.com.

SHOPS:

- **West Elm**, westelm.com. This shop has a great assortment of modern designs.
- **CB2**, cb2.com. The younger version of Crate & Barrell, for cool home accessories.
- **Fab**, fab.com. You can find some good pieces from top brands at reasonable prices here.

Top blogging tips:

- Don't get too caught up comparing yourself to others. The best bloggers are the ones who stay true to their own voice – to their own vision. Foster your own voice. Don't feel that you need to emulate somebody else's blog.
- If you're active on Twitter or Instagram, pick just one as your main outlet. Blogging has changed – there are lots of microblogging sites today and they're just as valid as having a bigger blog. It's still a way to share your ideas and thoughts.

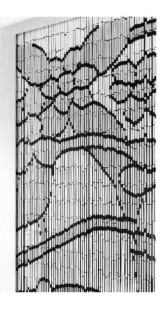

OPPOSITE Justina's 'jungalow' is filled with interesting ornaments picked up on her travels and is a flamboyant fusion of influences. 'My colourful Kilim rug is from Turkey,' she says. 'My Panton chairs are hand-me-downs from my grandma – I like objects that have history and a soul.'

LEFT In the kitchen, Justina displays pretty bottles and glass jars on shelves that are fixed across the window, so they catch the light. 'My goal was to make the kitchen look like a greenhouse,' she says.

BELOW Humorous touches give Justina's family home a relaxed, bohemian feel.'I love putting succulent plants in unexpected places,' says Justina. 'They're so low maintenance.'

Justina Blakeney Est. 1979

blog.justinablakeney.com

Designer and blogger Justina Blakeney lives with her husband, Jason, and baby daughter, Ida, in an eclectic bungalow – known affectionately as 'The Jungalow'. Filled with plants and treasures from her travels, it's a feast for the eyes – Turkish textiles, Mexican pottery, Swedish dolls, Nordic ceramics – layer upon layer of fascinating, handmade home accessories from all corners of the globe, stitched together to create a rich, colourful tapestry. In the laid-back world of this self-styled 'maximalist maker, mover, shaker' more is more. Here, botanicals go hand-in-hand with 'bling', leafy palms creep and climb across the corners of the rooms and Justina's signature 'wild decorating' style rules.

When Justina and Jason first saw the spacious garden of their rented home, they knew instantly that it was 'the one'. 'We just had a gut feeling,' remembers Justina. 'There were lots of people at the viewing, so we ran over to the landlord and made him an offer on the spot!'

The 1930s bungalow has plenty of character and space, providing the perfect canvas for Justina to introduce her trademark 'junaglow' look. 'A friend of mine coined the term in our previous home,' she explains. 'It suits my brand, my personality, my home and my style perfectly.'

jurger printers

mixed-media, ltd.
chicago

THIS PAGE Justina's living room is a joyful blend of colourful prints and patterns. The sofa is covered with vibrant, vintage textiles and the room has an eclectic, Bedouin-style feel. 'I love to watch the light filter in through the lace shawls that hang in the window,' she says.

In a world where minimalism and pared-back interiors are readily admired and celebrated, Justina's eclectic look offers a refreshing alternative. 'In the design world, there's so much hype about minimalism and simple beauty – but that's never been my vibe,' she says. 'One thing that sets me apart as a designer and a blogger is that I like having a lot of "stuff" around me. A jungle environment is thick and burgeoning with flowers, plants, animals and dense layers. That's how I like to live.'

Every room is filled with interesting objects. 'I collect artifacts,' says Justina. ' I studied anthropology so perhaps that's why I'm drawn to pieces that tell a story and connect people to their culture and roots.'

Justina's own background was a creative, nomadic one. Her parents took her travelling around the world and she developed her passion for eclectic, colourful design at a young age. 'I've always loved shopping at outdoor markets, even as a child,' she reveals. 'By the age of ten

LEFT The antique dresser in Justina's hallway was a bargain buy from a vintage shop in Los Angeles. 'It's become my mini succulent garden,' laughs Justina. 'I only water them once a month. I've had them in there for over a year already and they're still doing fine.'

OPPOSITE 'I love the contrast of shiny, slick glass with the wild plants outside,' says Justina. 'There are plants on the inside and plants on the outside – I like layers of glass and greenery.' Never one to shy away from bold colours, Justina has painted her kitchen woodwork in a deep, emerald green hue.

ABOVE Justina's signature hanging wooden plant holders proved so popular with her readers that she's teamed up with a carpenter and is now selling her own bespoke designs online. In the corner of her wooden-clad bedroom, she's created a comfortable window seat where she can read and covered it with colourful cushions/pillows.

LEFT Justina's bedroom is a riot of colour – filled with rich textiles in an array of prints and patterns. 'I collect brass birds,' she says. 'I find them in thrift stores and use them a lot in my styling work '

I'd been to Mexico several times, Indonesia, Europe and Israel; we moved around a lot.'

Her love of vintage textiles means every room of her home is filled with ornate patterns and sumptuous textures. 'It's the versatility of textiles that appeals most to me,' she reveals. 'You can make anything look good if you cover it with beautiful fabric. You can change the look of a sofa, a bed, a wall or a tabletop, to suit your mood.'

She also likes to 'travel virtually' through her textiles collection and changes the accessories in her home regularly. 'One night, I might want to recreate the feel of a Mexican feast, so I'll put a piece of Otomi fabric on the table. The next day, I might be in a Moroccan mood, so I'll throw a vintage wedding blanket from Marrakech over the sofa,' she explains.

Justina's online realm is equally colourful. 'The blog is just an extension of who I am,' she explains. 'I started blogging because I worked on a series of craft books and the publisher asked me to start a blog to support the launch and connect with readers. I was living in Italy and didn't even have internet access at the time. I had no idea about blogs. The internet wasn't a huge part of my life; I just used to check my emails in an internet café every now and again.'

THIS PAGE 'I bought the Suzani bed throw at the Grand Bazaar in Istanbul,' reveals Justina. Her amazing headboard is a vintage, mid-century, abstract, painted canvas, picked up in a thrift shop in Palm Desert. 'I bought two, but there were ten in the shop and I wish I'd bought all of them now!'

BELOW The beautiful antique dressing table in Justina's bedroom has had many incarnations. 'I've painted it various colours over the years, but at the moment it's bright turquoise,' says Justina. It's the perfect spot to display her favourite combination of 'botanicals and bling'; in this case, yellow Craspedia and an elegant, brass bird ornament.

When Justina moved to New York in 2008, she started to freelance for magazines and decided to combine her passions for writing, photography and design and take her blog a little more seriously. Today, she has a huge online following. 'Blogging is a dream job,' she says, smiling. 'I can travel, write, say and do what I want... I've worked for big magazine and book publishers before and sometimes felt that editors cramped my style.'

Blogging, she argues, has less 'red tape' than traditional print publishing. 'You can test the waters and see what resonates with your readers,' she continues. 'If you have an idea, you can just put it out there, show the world and get instant feedback. It's exciting.'

Now that she and Jason have baby Ida, Justina would like to move house again soon. 'We don't have much natural light here,' she complains. 'I'd love a home with huge windows. I'd also like a nice, clean, new kitchen. I love vintage features in every area of a house, except for the bathroom and kitchen.'

For Justina, 'The Jungalow' is more of a lifestyle than a geographical location, so it will be moving, too. 'My last home was a "jungalow" and my next home will be one, too. It sums up a way of decorating and living,' she says, already dreaming about her next creation.

RIGHT Justina expertly mixes natural materials such as bare wood and rattan with ornate, patterned accessories in her relaxed living room. Pottery bowls, Kilim rugs, Ikat-inspired accessories and thriving plants combine to create her signature – and refreshingly laid-back – 'jungalow' look. 'I'm drawn to artefacts from all over the world,' she says.

CENTRE RIGHT More is more in Justina's bedroom, where patterned, vintage textiles from all over the globe are piled high on the bed to create a nest-like retreat bursting with rich colours and prints. Justina has so many quilts that she has a whole cupboard in her living room for storing spares.

BOTTOM RIGHT 'When I bought these huge vases, I didn't know how big they were,' says Justina. 'When they arrived, the boxes were massive. That's what happens when you shop online sometimes. It's important to read the dimensions on listings – sometimes I get excited and just order too quickly!'

Justina loves:

- **Old Brand New**, oldbrandnewblog.com.
- **Satsuki Shibuya**, blog.satsukishibuya.com.
- **Moon to Moon**, frommoontomoon. blogspot.co.uk.

SHOPS:
- **Furbish Studio**, furbishstudio.com.
- **Gallivanting Girls**, etsy.com/shop/ GallivantingGirls.
- **Baba Souk**, babasouk.ca.
- **Loaded Trunk**, loadedtrunk.com.

Top blogging tips:

- Make your pictures big, at least 500 pixels across. You can't stretch them later because they'll go blurry and pixilated.
- It's might seem obvious, but it's overlooked a lot: get engaged in the community. Visit other blogs and comment on them. Have a presence on all the main platforms and engage with people who you respect and admire. Contact other bloggers and not just the biggest ones.
- Be careful about how you label and tag your posts. I use Pinterest to drive traffic, too. I have a large audience on there and I use a few little tricks to show people different content on my blog. Because a pizza recipe is the most popular post on my blog, instead of just pinning that post on Pinterest, I pinned from 'tags', so when somebody clicks on the Pinterest photo to get the recipe, instead of just getting that one recipe, they get all of my recipes. So they pin lots of them! It's really successful. Sometimes I re-pin things using a link to another tag, so instead of pinning from the tag for food or recipes, I pin the tag 'green', so then the pinner gets to access all my posts about the colour green. It's just a little helpful trick to increase traffic.
- Tailor your content. Pinterest is a huge traffic driver. The most popular things to share are recipes and DIY projects, so that's worth keeping in mind.
- Image-wise, horizontal format doesn't work as well on Pinterest as vertical format, so when you post on your blog, make sure that the first image you post is vertical so it shows up nice and big on Pinterest and not so tiny that people have to squint to see it.
- I host my blog on Wordpress. I started on Blogger but moved to Wordpress last year. Blogger was easy to use and intuitive. It's a really nice platform to start on, but I think it's possible to outgrow it, and I outgrew it. Wordpress is more difficult to personalise with limited programming skills, so I hired a designer to help me with that.

creating
your own
blog

'I'm the least techno-savvy person in the world, ever, and have no graphic design skills either. Luckily, you don't need to know any technical wizardry to start a blog!'

Niki Brantmark, My Scandinavian Home.

'You don't need to know any HTML programming code. I know little bits – like how to insert a hyperlink – but sites make it easy for beginners by providing all kinds of ready-to-use templates you can start with. As you progress you can learn how to personalise them more.'

Victoria Smith, SF Girl By Bay.

How to start your own blog

Are you inspired by the beautiful homes and blogs in this book? If you want to start your own blog to share your style and interior design ideas online, but are worried you don't have the right skills, don't despair – it's much easier than you might think, thanks to free design templates and readymade layouts. Follow our step-by-step guide and in no time at all, you'll have an online realm of your very own.

Get started

Think carefully about what you want to blog about and who your audience will be. Have a brainstorm to focus your ideas.

'Find a subject that you're passionate enough about to want to write about regularly.'
Rebecca Proctor, Futurustic.

'Do your research. Since there are so many blogs these days, it's important to make sure you're doing something that's different and not too similar to what's already out there, both in subject matter and aesthetic.'
Victoria Smith, SF Girl By Bay.

Think of a name

Ideally, your blog name should be easy to pronounce and spell – short, memorable and catchy. Run an internet search for your chosen blog name first, to check that nobody else has used it already and to ensure that you are not violating somebody else's trademark.

'Buy your own domain name before you start. I didn't do that but I wish I had – it would have made my life much easier later on'
Desireé Groenendal, Vosges Paris.

A 'domain name' is the web address of your blog. For example, bbc.co.uk is the domain name of the BBC (UK).

If you sign up to a free blog hosting platform, such as Blogger or WordPress, you will automatically be given a domain name such as myblogname.blogspot.com or myblogname.wordpress.com. This might not bother you, but if you would prefer a simpler, custom domain name such as myblogname.com, you need to purchase one, usually for a monthly or annual subscription fee.

A custom domain name is easier to remember and looks more professional, but it also has some practical advantages. If you want to move your blog to a new platform or your own web server in the future, it's much easier if your blog is not tied to a third-party address. Also, if you have your own domain name, all your existing visitors and back links will be preserved if you move your blog elsewhere.

Naming checklist

• Check that your chosen domain name is available for use by searching for it using a tool such as instantdomainsearch.com.

• If your chosen domain name is already registered to somebody else, you can find out who owns it at betterwhois.com.

• Register your chosen domain name with a reputable registrar service such as 123-reg.co.uk, godaddy.com, easydns.com or namecheap.com.

Choose a hosting platform

Hosts are online sites that will let you set up a blog, often for free or a small monthly fee. Which one you choose is a matter of personal preference, so shop around and explore a few options before committing. Generally, it's good to choose a large, reputable blogging platform for heightened security.

Blogger;
Blogger.com, free.

Used by: Desiree Groenendal, Vosges Paris; Niki Brantmark, My Scandinavian Home; Karine Köng, Bodie and Fou; Maria Carr, Dreamy Whites and Ilaria Chiaratti, IDA Interior Lifestyle.

'I've never had any problems with Blogger. It's very easy to use, so perfect for beginners.'
Desiree Groenendal, Vosges Paris.

'I logged into WordPress but found it too confusing. Blogger is simple by comparison.'
Niki Brantmark, My Scandinavian Home.

Blogger is Google's platform, so you need a Google or a Gmail account to get started. This also means that it integrates well with other Google blogging servces such as Feedburner, for RSS distribution, and all of your content is stored on the Google servers, so you don't have to worry about hosting fees, or bandwidth. Photos are uploaded through Google Picasa, which again is stored on your Google account and not on your own servers. You can easily personalize the background, header and basic design of your blog using a template editor tool.

Pros: Simple to use drag-and-drop template tools and free, custom domain name option.

Cons: Limited design customization options.

WordPress;

WordPress.com (and WordPress.org), free.

Used by: Justina Blakeney, Justina Blakeney Est.1979; Jonathan Lo, Happy Mundane; Jill Macnair and Ros Anderson, My Friend's House; Jane Schouten, All The Luck In The World; Victoria Smith, SF Girl By Bay and Rebecca Proctor, Futurustic.

'I started on Blogger but moved to WordPress last year. Blogger is easy to use and intuitive so it's a really nice platform to start on, but I think it's possible to outgrow it, and I outgrew it.'
Justina Blakeney, Justina Blakeney Est.1979

'WordPress blogs can be customised more than blogs on some of the other platforms. I was on Blogger

for a few years but my layouts were simple at that time anyway. Now I like being able to customise my design more.' *Jonathan Lo, Happy Mundane.*

There are two WordPress options: Wordpress.com and Wordpress.org. If you sign up to the free hosted WordPress.com service, you will automatically get a myblogname.wordpress.com domain name, but you can pay extra to use your own custom domain name. If you sign up to the Wordpress.org version, you can host WordPress on your own servers and have much more control over the look of the blog – you can edit themes, add plug-ins and hack code. But all this requires technical skill, so if you're a beginner, stick to the Wordpress.com option.

Pros: Exciting customisation options, forums filled with advice, plenty of plug-ins to choose from and useful built-in traffic statistics.

Cons: Can be a bit confusing for beginners and some complain that it's complicated to use.

Typepad;

Typepad.com, from £5.60/$8.95 per month.

Used by: Joy Cho, Oh Joy!

'When I started blogging, there were only a few platforms available. For me, it's been great for many years. You can start on a very basic version and then easily incorporate custom features at a later date.'
Joy Cho, Oh Joy!

Favoured by many long-time bloggers. Where users of WordPress have to rely on huge community forums for advice and help, with TypePad, you can open a help ticket and get a personal response from a customer service advisor within 24 hours.

Pros: Unlimited storage, easy-to-use tools, off-the-peg designs, as well as plenty of options for customization, and great customer support.

Cons: It's not free and if you want to modify the CSS script for style sheets in order to customize the appearance of your blog, you have to subscribe to the Unlimited package at an additional cost. The functionality add-ons are not exhaustive.

Also worth considering
Tumblr;

Tumblr.com, free.

Good for: Visual, image-led blog posts and a sense of community – users can easily interact with one another and share content.

Map your domain name to your blog

If you have decided to buy your own custom domain name such as myblogname.com or myblogname.net, search for an online tutorial on your chosen blogging platform, Wordpress, Blogger etc., to follow in order to connect, or map, your custom domain name to your blog. Some hosting platforms, like Blogger, will let you do this for free, while others, such as Wordpress, require a small annual fee.

Get your images right

Any design blog needs beautiful images. Whether you want to share your own photos, other people's, or a mixture of the two, you'll need some basic tools and skills.

'You live and learn. I didn't know how to re-size images when I started out. To begin with, I was uploading enormous, high resolution digital image files that would take literally a whole day because our internet connection was so slow. It drove me crazy. Now I re-size all of my images and reduce the file sizes before I upload them. It saves a lot of time!'
Maria Carr, Dreamy Whites.

'Make sure that all your images are the same size. Visually, it really helps. When images on a blog are all different sizes, it boggles my brain – I can't even read blogs that look like that! When I started, all my images were different sizes and it's hard to go back now to re-size all the images in those early posts, so get it sorted before you start.

Image-wise, horizontal format doesn't work as well on Pinterest as vertical format, so when you post on your blog, make sure that the first image you include in a post is vertical so it shows up nice and big.'
Justina Blakeney, Justina Blakeney Est. 1979.

Image checklist

• Re-size your images before you upload them to your blogging platform and insert them into your posts. Use an image-editing tool within your blogging platform

if there is one; an online tool such as Pixlr, Pixlr.com, or Gimp, Gimp.org; or paid-for software such as Photoshop Elements by Adobe.

- Experiment until you find the best width (in pixels) for images in your blog posts and use that as a template. Blog post columns are usually around 500–600 pixels wide so use that as a starting point.
- Don't upload images that are high resolution, such as 300 dpi (dots per inch), and enormous in size as they will take too long to upload and display as well as take up precious storage space on your own or host server. Instead, stick to smaller images that are around 72 dpi in resolution.

Grow your audience

Now you've set up a blog and started to post, you might want to attract as many followers as possible. However, this isn't every blogger's goal.

'People blog for different reasons. Some people just need an outlet and they don't really care if anybody reads it. That's fine too.'
Jonathan Lo, Happy Mundane.

'Don't stress. It can be easy to worry about growing an audience, but if you are creative, authentic and are doing something different, people will soon tune in. When you start blogging, drive traffic by telling everyone you know. That includes your family and friends as well as other bloggers you admire. You can't sit there and expect people to find you via a Google search, so let everyone know you're out there.'
Joy Cho, Oh Joy!'

Connect with other bloggers

Use tools such as Bloglovin, Bloglovin.com, or Feedly, Feedly.com, to organise and keep track of your favourite blogs so you can read them regularly and comment on them, always including a link back to your own blog.

'Be open and comment on other bloggers' blogs, then your network will grow organically.'
Ilaria Chiaratti, IDA Interior Lifestyle.

'Don't just contact the biggest bloggers. A lot of new bloggers comment on the biggest blogs in order to try to build up their brand and increase traffic, but I think there's a real missed opportunity to comment on medium-sized blogs that have fewer readers, or blogs that you just genuinely love. These smaller blogs might not have huge audiences, but the bloggers

behind them will probably have a bit more time to read comments, click on your link, find out who you are and respond.'

Justina Blakeney, Justina Blakeney Est.1979.

Respond to your readers

Keep track of your traffic using your platform's built-in statistics tool or Google Analytics – you'll need a Google account to use this function, see google.com/analytics – and study where your visitors are coming from and what posts are the most popular, so you know what to focus on.

'Tailor your content. Pinterest is a huge traffic driver. The most popular things I share on Pinterest are recipes and DIY projects, so that's worth keeping in mind. My house tour post is popular, but the most popular post ever on my blog is an avocado and egg, breakfast pizza recipe – strange, but true!'

Justina Blakeney, Justina Blakeney Est.1979.

'My DIY posts are always popular with readers but the most popular post I ever did was the most random, too. I shared a photo of magnified grains of sand that looked like sea shells. That got picked up by somebody who had a huge following on Tumblr and I got loads of hits. You can never predict what will happen. You never know who's looking.'

Jonathan Lo, Happy Mundane.

Have a presence on all social media platforms

Use tools like Instagram, Pinterest, Twitter, Facebook, Google+, LinkedIn to promote your blog, connect with your audience and interact with other bloggers.

'Synch all your social media accounts to save time and energy. When I post on my blog, it automatically updates my Twitter and Instagram feeds too, with links to the post.'

Rebecca Proctor, Futurustic.

'I use Pinterest to drive traffic to my blog as I have a large audience on there. I tag and label all my blog posts as I go. Because a specific pizza recipe is, randomly, the most popular post on my blog, instead of just pinning that post on Pinterest, I pinned from tags, so when somebody clicks on the Pinterest photo to get the recipe, instead of just getting that one recipe, they get all of my recipes. Then they start browsing and pin lots of them. It's really successful. Sometimes I re-pin things using a link to another tag, so instead of pinning the pizza image from a tag for food or recipes, I pin from the tag 'green', so then the pinner gets access to all my posts about the colour green. It's a helpful trick to increase traffic and pins.'

Justina Blakeney, Justina Blakeney Est.1979.

Master search engine optimization

Search Engine Optimization (SEO) is what you can do to make sure your blog gets the best possible results in search engine listings.

Identify relevant key words and phrases on which you will concentrate for getting a good ranking for your website. Think about phrases and words that people are likely to type into search engines to access content that's related to your blog subject matter. Incorporate these words into the text in your blog post titles and content as much as possible without going overboard and making your posts annoying or strange. Be subtle.

When you're posting on your blog, label all your posts with keywords and tags, behind-the-scene, in the keywords area of your content management system (CMS) blog-post editing tool. Enter at least 20 words per post, separating them with commas.

Remember to name your image files with search engine-friendly words too. An image with the file name: 'IMG_123' won't get picked up easily, so a more specific, descriptive file name, such as 'Pink_floral_wallpaper', is better.

'**Create a strong identity – it gives you a great brand. Own your language, too. 'Jungalow' is a made up word, so when people Google it, 90 per cent of the content that comes up is related to me. It's important to find your voice, then find your own words. I have an Excel spreadsheet of keywords I use over and over again – language that is a good representation of my brand. That's how I grow my brand and spread it. I deliberately use phrases like 'decorate wild', or 'thrifting with Justina' on my blog and also on social media – such as in hash tags on Twitter – in order to build up a solid brand around who I am as a person, a blogger and a designer.'**
Justina Blakeney, Justina Blakeney Est.1979.

Get into a rhythm

Whether you post every day or every week, having a regular posting schedule is crucial. It might help to plan in advance and post regular features on the same day each week, so your readers know when to visit and what to expect.

'**Consistency is really important so people know when to look at your blog. If you post once every four months, nobody will ever know when you're posting and your readers will lose interest.'**
Jonathan Lo, Happy Mundane.

'**Organise your time and fit blogging in around your other commitments. I often blog in the evening, in time that was previously wasted.'**
Jill Macnair, My Friend's House.

Just be yourself

It's easy to compare your blog to other blogs, but to stand out, you just need to do your own thing. Find your niche, then specialise and create an online realm that reflects you, not somebody else.

'**Stay true to yourself and find your own voice. Don't emulate other blogs. Be natural. The more your blog reflects you, the better it is.'**
Victoria Smith, SF Girl By Bay.

'**Do it your way. Don't get distracted by other great blogs. It's easy to feel as though you should be doing this or that, but just do something original that's your own. Stay true to your personal path.'**
Jill Macnair, My Friend's House.

Golden advice from the experts

'Credit others and be respectful. Always mention and link to photographers and stylists if you feature their work on your blog.'
Karine Köng, Bodie and Fou.

'A professional designer can make your blog look great. If you can't afford one, you could trade skills – if you're a good photographer or a great writer, you can help them in return for them helping you. I'm all in favour of a bit of bartering to get help. It's a good way to make things happen without having to spend a lot of money.'
Victoria Smith, S F Girl By Bay.

'Take your own photos and create your own fresh content. That's crucial.'
Desiree Groenendal, Vosges Paris.

'Don't view blogging as a one-way medium to broadcast yourself. Become part of an online community and share your thoughts, but ask for ideas, too.'
Niki Brantmark, My Scandinavian Home.

'Get involved. Attend blogging meet-up events and find out who is behind the screen. Networking is crucial both online and offline.'
Ilaria Chiaratti, IDA Interior Lifestyle.

'Be personal. People like it when you engage, but you don't have to share everything in your life.'
Victoria Smith, S F Girl By Bay.

Glossary

Blog
Derived from the term 'weblog', meaning a series of chronological, dated posts.

CMS
Content Management System is a user-friendly website that a blog or website owner can use to manage and edit a blog or site, without needing to use code.

Domain
The web address of your blog or website.

Hosting
The virtual space that you 'rent' on the internet, where your blog or website is stored.

HTML
Hypertext Markup Language is the basic code for programming websites.

Hyperlink
An image or a piece of text that links to another web page on the internet.

Plugin
A tool you can add to your blog to give it an extra ability or function.

RSS
A stream of content that readers can use to read their favourite blogs in a feed.

Search engine

A tool, such as Google, that searches content on the internet for you.

SEO

Search Engine Optimisation refers to methods you can implement to ensure that your website or blog ranks highly in search engine listings, maximising traffic.

Social media

Services such as Twitter and Facebook that allow users to chat, interact, network and share information and images.

Widget

A sidebar tool or element that provides extra information or a useful function, such as a search bar or a list of recent tweets.

Sources

colour fun

Baba Souk
babasouk.ca

CB2
451 Broadway, New York, NY 10013, USA
+1 (630) 388 4555
cb2.com

Fab
+44 (0)800 7645 3546
fab.com

Furbish Studio
312 West Johnson Street,
Raleigh, NC 27603, USA
+1 (919) 521 4981
furbishstudio.com

Gallivanting Girls
etsy.com/shop/GallivantingGirls

Loaded Trunk
loadedtrunk.com

West Elm
112 West 18th Street, New York , NY 10011, USA
+1 (800) 1500 4444
westelm.com

homespun

Camp Cirrus
etsy.com/shop/campcirrus

Een Nieuw Avontuur
eennieuwavontuur.com

La Cerise Sur Le Gâteau
+33 3 89 50 38 58
shop.lacerisesurlegateau.fr

Mae Engelgeer
Nieuwevaart 3 1.09, 1018 AA, Amsterdam
+31 (0)6 10 89 79 14
mae-engelgeer.nl

Nina Invorm
etsy.com/shop/Ninainvorm

Snug Studio
etsy.com/uk/shop/snugstudio

pared back

Chez Les Voisins
chezlesvoisins.fr

Katharina Berggreen
kathapult.bigcartel.com

Love Warriors of Sweden
Efraim Dahlinsväg 6,
SE–128 64 Sköndal, Sweden
+55 6793 7346
lovewarriors.se

Lovely & Co.
Unit 5, Davigdor Mews,
Hove, East Sussex, BN3 1RF, UK
lovelyandcompany.co.uk

L'Atelier du Petit Parc
19 Allée Baco, 44000 Nantes, France
+33 (0)2 4944 1965
atelierdupetitparc.fr

La Maison d'Anna G
lamaisondannag.com

Les Petits Bohemes
lespetitsbohemes.bigcartel.com

Merci
111 Boulevard Beaumarchais,
75003 Paris, France
+33 (0)1 8005 2967
merci-merci.com

Saana Ja Olli
Louhenkatu 5 as 2, 20100 Turku, Finland
saanajaolli.com

Stilleben
+45 3391 1131
stillebenshop.com

VT Wonen Shop
033 7544100
vtwonenshop.nl

retro chic

Between Dog and Wolf
betweendogandwolf.co.uk

Factory20
Abingdon, Virginia, VA 24210, USA
+1 (703) 655 8831
factory20.com

Ferm Living
+45 7022 7523
fermliving.com

Future and Found
116 A Fortess Road, London, NW5 2HL, UK
+44 (0)20 7267 4772
futureandfound.com

J.Crew
165 Regent Street London W1B 4AD, UK; and,
10 Columbus Circle, New York, NY 10019, USA
jcrew.com

Leif
leifshop.com

Mini Rodini
Klippgatan 11, 116 35 Stockholm, Sweden
+46 8 124 539 62
minirodini.com

Papa Stour
papastour.com

Society
1 Via Palermo, 20121 Milan, Italy
+39 02 7208 0453
societylimonta.com

Serendipity
81–83 Rue du Cherche-Midi,
75006 Paris, France
+33 (0)1 42 22 12 18
serendipity.fr

rustic

Anthropologie
158 Regent Street, London, W1B 5SW, UK; and,
375 West Broadway, New York, NY 10012, USA
+44 (0)800 0026 8476
anthropologie.com

Couverture & The Garbstore
188 Kensington Park Road, London, W11 2ES, UK
+44 (0)20 7229 2178
couvertureandthegarbstore.com

Fine Little Day
Fine Little Day, Stigbergsliden 5,
414 63 Gothenburg, Sweden
shop.finelittleday.com

Herriott Grace
shop.herriottgrace.com

Maison Rêve
+1 (415) 383 9700
maisonreve.com

The New Craftsmen
thenewcraftsmen.myshopify.com

Sadie Olive
sadieolive.com

general

A Rum Fellow
+44 (0)20 8245 6779
arumfellow.com

Angie Lewin
angielewin.co.uk

Eleanor Pritchard
+ 44 (0) 208 692 2544
eleanorpritchard.com

Etsy
etsy.com

Farrow & Ball
Uddens Estate, Wimborne, Dorset, BH21 7NL, UK
+44 (0)1202 876 141
farrow-ball.com

Florence Broadhurst
florencebroadhurst.com.au

H&M
hm.com

Heath Ceramics
+1 (415) 332 3732
heathceramics.com

IKEA
ikea.com

Jorg Steigerhout
jorg-steigerhout.nl

Katia di Maglie
artoleria.com

Kingdom Interiors
The Long Barn, Mitre Farm Business Park,
Corse Lawn, Gloucestershire, GL19 4NG, UK
kingdominteriors.co.uk

Liberty of London
Regent Street, London, W1B 5AH, UK
+44 (0)20 7734 1234
liberty.co.uk

Lilly's Lightbox Company
Headland Studios 23, Headland Way,
Lingfield, Surrey, RH7 6DH, UK
lillyslightboxcompany.com

Madeline Weinrib
126 5th Avenue, New York, NY 10011, USA
+1 (212) 414 5978
madelineweinrib.com

Marimekko
Puusepänkatu 4, 00880 Helsinki, Finland
+358 9 758 71
marimekko.com

Morsø
morso.co.uk

mt masking tape
www.masking-tape.jp

PiP Studio
+31 (0) 343 439409
pipstudio.com

Suki Cheema
+44 (0)20 3560 6299
sukicheema.com

Target
+1 (800) 591 3869
target.com

Tate
+44 (0)20 7887 8869
shop.tate.org.uk

Toast
+44 (0)844 557 0460
toast.co.uk

Picture credits

All photography by Rachel Whiting.

Endpapers The family home of Justina Blakeney in Los Angeles; **1** Jonathan Lo; **2** The home of Maria Carr of www.dreamywhitesonline.com; **4** Victoria Smith, editor of www.sfgirlbybay.com; **5** The home of interior journalist and blogger Jill Macnair in London; **7 above left** The home of interior journalist and blogger Jill Macnair in London; **7 above right** The home of Jane Schouten of All the Luck in the World blog; **7 below** The family home of Rebecca Proctor in Cornwall www.futurusticblog.com; **8–19** Niki Brantmark of My Scandinavian Home; **20–29** Karine Köng, founder and Creative Director of online concept store BODIE and FOU, www.bodieandfou.com; **30–39** The home of Desiree of VosgesParis.com in Rhenen; **40–51** The family home of Rebecca Proctor in Cornwall www.futurusticblog.com; **52–61** The home of Maria Carr of www.dreamywhitesonline.com; **62–71** Victoria Smith, editor sfgirlbybay.com; **72–81** The home of interior journalist and blogger Jill Macnair in London; **82–91** Joy Cho – designer and blogger of Oh Joy!; **92–105** The home of Jane Schouten of All the Luck in the World blog; **106–115** The home of Ilaria of IDA Interior Lifestyle in Eindhoven; **116–127** Jonathan Lo; **128–137** The family home of Justina Blakeney in Los Angeles; **138–139** Jonathan Lo; **140** Joy Cho – designer and blogger of Oh Joy!; **141** The home of Ilaria of IDA Interior Lifestyle in Eindhoven; **143** The family home of Justina Blakeney in Los Angeles; **145** Karine Köng, founder and Creative Director of online concept store BODIE and FOU www.bodieandfou.com; **146** The family home of Rebecca Proctor in Cornwall www.futurusticblog.com; **148** The home of interior journalist and blogger Jill Macnair in London; **149** Jonathan Lo; **150 above left** The home of Desiree of VosgesParis.com in Rhenen; **150 above right** Niki Brantmark of My Scandinavian Home; **150 below left** The home of Ilaria of IDA Interior Lifestyle in Eindhoven; **150 below right** Karine Köng, founder and Creative Director of online concept store BODIE and FOU www.bodieandfou.com; **151** The home of Ilaria of IDA Interior Lifestyle in Eindhoven; **152–155** The home of interior journalist and blogger Jill Macnair in London; **157** Niki Brantmark of My Scandinavian Home; **160** The home of interior journalist and blogger Jill Macnair in London.

Business credits

Ellie Tennant
Interiors journalist, stylist and author
+44 (0) 7815 869370
www.ellietennant.com

Jane Schouten
All the Luck in the World
Blog.alltheluckintheworld.nl
pages 7 above right, 92–105.

Karine Köng
Bodie and Fou
www.bodieandfou.com
pages 20–29, 145, 150 below right.

Maria Carr
Dreamy Whites
www.dreamywhitesonline.com
pages 2, 52–61.

Rebecca Proctor
Futurustic
www.futurusticblog.com
and
www.guineatruckle.co.uk
pages 7 below, 40–51, 146.

Jonathan Lo
Happy Mundane
www.happymundane.com
www.theoctopian.com
www.j3productions.com
pages 1, 116–127, 138–139, 149.

Ilaria Chiaratti
IDA Interior Lifestyle
www.idainteriorlifestyle.com
pages 106–115, 141, 150 below left, 151.

Justina Blakeney
Justina Blakeney Est. 1979
designer, blogger and stylist
blog.justinablakeney.com
Endpapers, 128–137, 143.

Jill Macnair
My Friend's House
www.myfriendshouse.co.uk
and
www.jillmacnair.com
pages 5, 7 above left, 72–81, 148, 152–155, 160.

Niki Brantmark
My Scandinavian Home
www.myscandinavianhome.blogspot.com.uk
pages 8–19, 150 above right, 157.

Joy Deangdeelert Cho
Oh Joy!
www.ohjoy.blogs.com
pages 82–91, 140.

Victoria Smith
SF Girl by Bay
www.sfgirlbybay.com
pages 4, 62–71.

Desiree Groenendal
Vosges Paris
www.vosgesparis.blogspot.com
pages 30–39, 150 above left.

Index

Figures in *italics* indicate captions.

Acknowledgments

'The ornament of a house is the friends who frequent it.'

Ralph Waldo Emerson, essayist and poet (1803-1882)

Firstly, I would like to thank the brilliant Rachel Whiting for her stunning photography and excellent company travelling the globe. It was a pleasure and an honour to work with such a talented professional who is also a lovely person.

I'm very grateful to the whole team at Ryland Peters & Small for commissioning my idea in the first place and for working so hard to make the whole production process run smoothly from beginning to end.

Of course, this book would not have been possible without the support of the twelve friendly design bloggers who welcomed us into their homes. Their kindness and generosity was overwhelming and they were an absolute delight to work with.

I'd also like to thank my dear friends and family for all their love and support, especially my parents Mike and Pippa, who have always nurtured and encouraged me in whatever I do, my sister Sarah, my in-laws Janet and David, who have been running an impressive PR campaign in rural Worcestershire, my publishing gurus Lucy and Maddy, all the 'Henry's Angels' and my fantastic husband Rob, who is everything.

Finally, I'd like to thank you for reading this book! I hope you enjoyed it and found some fresh ideas for your home along the way.